3-Dimensional Earth

WRITTEN BY:
Sean Connolly

CONSULTANT:
Dr David Munro
ROYAL SCOTTISH GEOGRAPHICAL SOCIETY

PANORAMIC MAPS BY:
Alan Collinson Design

MARSHALL PUBLISHING · LONDON

A Marshall Edition
Conceived, edited and designed by
Marshall Editions Ltd
The Orangery
161 New Bond Street
London W1S 2UF
www.marshallpublishing.com

First published in the UK in 2000
by Marshall Publishing Ltd

Copyright © 2000 Marshall Editions
Developments Ltd

Originated in Italy by Articolor
Printed and bound in Italy
by De Agostini

10 9 8 7 6 5 4 3 2 1

ISBN 1 84028 485 4

Editor:	Kate Maitland Smith
Design Manager:	Ralph Pitchford
Editorial Manager:	Kate Phelps
Publishing Director:	Linda Cole
Art Director:	Simon Webb
Production:	Amanda Mackie and
	Nikki Ingram
Picture Researcher:	Antonella Mauro
Indexer:	Hilary Bird

Cover photography: front t Digital Vision,
cl PowerStock, cr Francois Gohier/Ardea,
bl The Stock Market, br Rinie Van Meurs/Bruce
Coleman; back l The Stock Market, r Francois
Gohier/Ardea.
Cover artwork: front map Alan Collinson Design;
back tl Peter Bull, compass Rob Jakeway, South
America maps Alan Collinson Design, cr Peter
Bull, bl world map Ralph Pitchford.

Contents

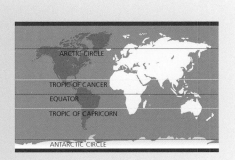

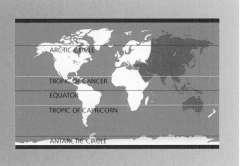
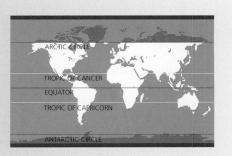

Exploring our World

▲ **FINDING YOUR WAY AROUND**
Throughout this book, a small map like the one above gives you a conventional view of the world (this is the view maps usually give us). The continent or continents featured on each spread are shown in red so that you always know what part of the world you are looking at.

▼ Because you are "flying around" the maps and seeing the continents and oceans from different angles, there is always a compass to show you in which direction you are looking. The red needle of the compass always points to north. (*See also opposite page.*) Many of the maps focus on only a part of a continent, so a conventional map of the same area is provided in the bottom-left corner of the page to show you where you are and how the area is normally shown.

Only in the late 1960s were we at last able to see and study the Earth from space. This photograph was taken from the Luna Module during the Apollo 11 mission to fly to the Moon in 1969.

Ordinary maps show you where different places are. But imagine what it would be like to have your own personal space shuttle to whoosh you around the world so you could see places for yourself. You could soar up into the atmosphere and look at entire continents and oceans laid out beneath you. You might swoop down and hover over the tip of South America and see the tall peaks of the Andes mountains stretching off into the distance, where the Amazon River begins its course down into the Amazon Basin. Or you could whizz to northern Africa to see the different landscapes of the vast Sahara Desert. In fact, you could go anywhere and look at the Earth from wherever you chose. This atlas cannot give you a real shuttle, but it lets you imagine you are soaring over the Earth.

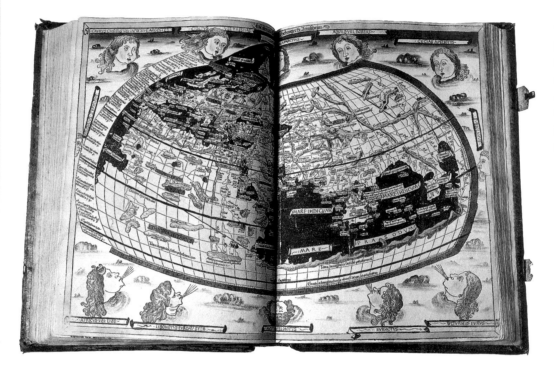

◀ *The ancient Greek geographer, Ptolemy, produced the information to make a world map in AD 150. His map is recreated in this woodcut of 1482. Ptolemy's map shows only those parts of the world that he knew, which is why there is a lot of detail around the Mediterranean Sea. The heads around the map represent the main winds.*

Early mapping

People have been trying to map the world for more than 2,500 years. The earliest maps showed only those areas of the world that the mapmakers knew, which were usually only very small sections of the Earth, and they were not very accurate. Many people still believed that the Earth was flat and that a ship could sail off the edge or meet dragons in some as yet unmapped area. Some maps were based on Christian ideas about the world, and the 13th-century Mappa Mundi, or "Map of the World", shows Jerusalem at the centre. Other maps used information gathered along trading routes to lands in Asia, and the sizes of these lands were often exaggerated.

The Earth from space

It is only in the last 30 years or so that people have really been able to see the world as a whole. Space missions, launched either from the United States of America or the former Soviet Union, have sent astronauts as far as the Moon and back again. Unlike the first mapmakers, who only saw one part of the world, these astronauts have been able to see the whole Earth in space. In the same period many unmanned satellites have been launched into orbit around the Earth. They carry equipment that can photograph every part of the Earth's surface and even provide information about water temperature, climate and volcanic activity.

Changing views in 3-Dimensional Earth

On ordinary maps, the world always looks flat and north is always at the top. This way of showing places is so familiar that it is easy for us to forget that the world is not really like that. The Earth is a globe, not flat, and everything on it has height, width and depth. Just as your house looks different if you look at it from different angles (from down the street or up in a plane, for example) so, if you flew high enough, you could see continents and oceans from all kinds of viewpoints. You would see how high the mountains are and how deep the valleys are. You would see where the land rises into a plateau or where vast rivers have cut steep-sided gorges. In this atlas, all the maps show you the continents and oceans in a new and revealing way, as if you were actually flying around them. To show you how our maps work, the illustration on the right takes you on a flying tour around North America. See how the shape of the land seems to change as it is viewed from different directions and angles.

Mapping the globe

A globe is the only truly accurate map of the world. But globes are not very practical for carrying around, so most maps are drawn on flat paper. Imagine peeling an orange a quarter at a time and laying the quarters of peel down flat. The best flat map of the world would "peel" away the surface of the globe and lay the pieces out flat in the same way. This method would be accurate but it would leave big gaps on the paper, like the gaps between the segments of orange peel. Mapmakers try to show the world as accurately as the imaginary "orange peel segments" but without confusing people with the spaces between the segments. The different ways of drawing the Earth's curved surface onto a flat piece of paper are called map projections.

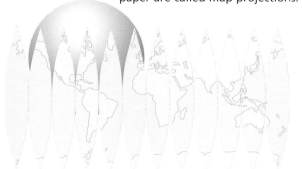

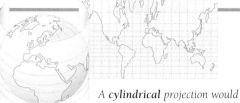

*A **cylindrical** projection would be made if a piece of paper was wrapped all the way around the equator. This method is the most common, although only the parts of the globe near the equator show up as they really are – the areas farther away are distorted.*

*A second projection, called a **planar** projection, shows how the Earth would look if a piece of paper was laid over just one point of the globe, such as a pole.*

▲ *The "orange peel" view of the Earth is sometimes called **Goode's** Projection. Although the sizes and shapes of the continents and oceans are accurate when the "peel" is attached to the globe, there are huge gaps across them when the pieces are laid out flat.*

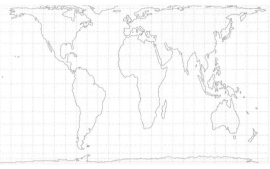

*A **Mercator** Projection is a cylindrical projection that has been adjusted to make the shapes of the land masses farther from the equator more accurate but it distorts the true sizes.*

*A **Peters'** Projection is a cylindrical projection that has been adjusted to show the true sizes of the land masses, but the shapes have to be stretched to do this.*

The maps in this book

Many satellites in orbit around the Earth carry cameras and other equipment to collect detailed images of the Earth's surface. Once fed into computers, these images create very accurate maps of every part of the world. The maps in this atlas are produced by computer, which allows us to build up 3-dimensional pictures of the surface. The heights of the land have been exaggerated so that we can still "see" towering mountains, deep valleys and immense seas and deserts, even when vast lands are reduced to the size of pages in a book. And we can "fly" around our maps by turning the images. We can also colour the maps to show additional information, such as climate.

1. This is the view from the northwest, over Alaska, looking southeast along the Rocky Mountains and over the Great Prairies towards the Caribbean Sea.

8. This is the view from the north, high over the Arctic Circle, looking south towards the Gulf of Mexico.

7. This is the view from the northeast, over Greenland, looking southwest over Hudson Bay towards Mexico.

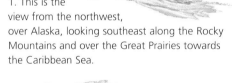

2. This is the view from the west, over the Pacific Ocean, looking east over the Rocky Mountains and the Great Prairies towards the east coast and the Atlantic Ocean.

NORTH AMERICA

6. This is the view from the east, over the Atlantic Ocean, looking west over the Great Prairies towards the Rocky Mountains.

3. This is the view from the southwest, over the Pacific Ocean, looking northeast over the Rocky Mountains and the Great Prairies to Hudson Bay and Baffin Island.

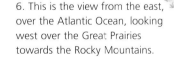

5. This is the view from the southeast, over the Caribbean Sea, looking northwest over the Appalachian Mountains towards Alaska in the distance.

4. This is the view from the south, over Mexico, looking north along the Rocky Mountains towards Canada.

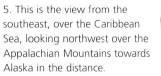

A Changing Planet

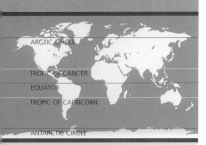

• THE EARTH
Age:
4.6 billion years
Tilt (from vertical):
23.5 degrees
Diameter (pole to pole):
12,713 km (7,883 miles)
Diameter (through the equator):
12,756 km (7,909 miles)
Circumference (around the equator):
40,074 km (24,846 miles)
Average diameter of core:
6,964 km (4,318 miles)
Average thickness of mantle:
2,800 km (1,736 miles)
Average thickness of crust:
20 km (12 miles)
Surface area:
510 million sq km
(196 million sq miles)
Percentage of surface covered by water: 71 percent
Average surface temperature:
14°C (57°F)

We see only a tiny part of the whole Earth – the surface, or crust, we live on. This crust extends all around the planet as a sort of wrapping. It lies beneath the continents and the oceans. But this "wrapping" is affected by what happens inside the Earth, where powerful forces, caused by high temperature and pressure, are constantly at work. Over the nearly 5 billion years since the Earth was formed in space, these forces have created both the continents and the oceans as well as islands, lakes and seas. But the Earth's history is far from over, and if this book were written several million years from now, all the maps would be different. The constant creation, reshaping and destruction of lands and seas would have created new landmarks while others would have been lost forever.

▲ **Fossils of marine animals** such as ammonites are scattered across a valley floor high up in the Himalayas. Millions of years ago this mountain valley formed the bed of the Indian Ocean. The fossils provide evidence of how the Himalayas formed.

A look within

The Earth is made up of layers (*right*). The outer layer – called the crust – is the thinnest of these layers; relative to their sizes, the Earth's crust is hardly thicker than an egg's shell. Immediately beneath the crust is the outer mantle, where rocks are sometimes molten (or partially melted) and can push through the crust to the surface. The inner mantle is a solid layer and the material within it becomes denser as it nears the centre. The two layers of the core are made of nickel and iron. The outer core is molten, but the immense pressure at the Earth's centre means that the inner core remains solid.

solid iron core
MOLTEN OUTER CORE
INNER MANTLE
OUTER MANTLE
crust

Volcanoes

Hot molten rock (called lava), ash, gas, steam and other materials are constantly pushing upwards from the Earth's outer mantle towards the crust. The intense heat of the Earth's interior causes these materials to expand. Sometimes they find a crack in the crust that is wide enough for the material to flow through steadily to the surface. Beneath other parts of the crust they build up pressure and temperature until they erupt with a powerful explosion. Any natural opening through which these materials escape is called a volcano.

Hurricane winds sweep across an exposed coast. The Earth's powerful forces are not confined to the layers beneath the surface. Two non-solid layers lie outside the solid crust of the Earth. The hydrosphere is the layer of water on the surface. It includes lakes, rivers and seas as well as the oceans. Above the Earth is the atmosphere, the layer of gases that includes the air we breathe. The air and oceans have currents, caused largely by the rotation of the Earth and the huge differences in temperature between the equator and the poles. Sometimes these currents can create destructive storms such as hurricanes (also known as typhoons and cyclones).

ash and steam

◄ **In a typical volcano,** magma builds up in a central chamber. It finds its way to the surface through a central vent, erupting when it reaches the top. Lava flows down the side, eventually hardening to form the familiar cone shape. Sometimes the lava finds its way through side vents in the cone.

central vent
cone
side vent
side chamber
lava
separate cone formed by side vent
layers of hardened lava from earlier eruptions
magma
central chamber

▲ **Scientists take measurements** of temperature, the speed of lava flow and the length of a volcanic eruption to learn more about when and where we can expect new volcanic activity. Sometimes, these scientists must fly dangerously close to the eruption.

   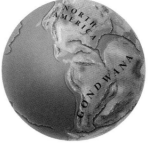  

| 620 million years ago | 320 million years ago | 240 million years ago | 130 million years ago | 65 million years ago | 45 million years ago |

Plate tectonics

Imagine that the Earth is a hardboiled egg that you just dropped. If you put the pieces of shell back together, they would form a sort of jigsaw puzzle covering the surface of the egg. The Earth's crust is rather like such a thin-shelled jigsaw puzzle. The pieces of "shell" are called plates, but these plates are slowly moving. This structure and movement is called plate tectonics. Forces at work inside the Earth push new rock upwards, through cracks between the plates and this causes the plates themselves to slide across the Earth's surface. Many of the Earth's continents lie on single plates, and it is the movement of these plates that is sometimes called "continental drift". Over the course of many millions of years the continents slide and turn, sometimes merging with other continents and at other times breaking apart.

▲ **The Earth's continents** have changed over millions of years. Look at a modern map and you will see that the east coast of South America and the west coast of Africa fit together like pieces of a jigsaw puzzle. Studies of rock and mountain formations proved that these continents were once linked. This "supercontinent" gradually broke apart and the pieces drifted across the Earth's surface to form the continents as we now know them.

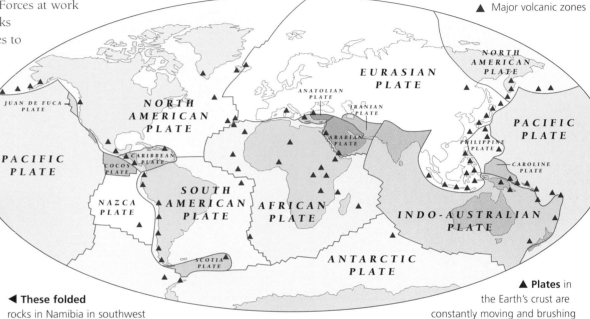

▲ Major volcanic zones

◀ **These folded** rocks in Namibia in southwest Africa once lay at the bottom of the Atlantic Ocean. The movement of plates pushed the oceanic crust almost back on itself to form these mountains. Each curved band in the rock was once a flat layer of the seabed.

▲ **Plates** in the Earth's crust are constantly moving and brushing against each other. This movement accounts for nearly all the earthquakes that occur on Earth (*see page 15*). Most of the openings for volcanic activity are along the edges of the plates, where the crust is weakest.

Mountain building

The movement of plates creates most of the Earth's mountains (*see right*). When an oceanic plate collides with a continental plate, the thinner oceanic crust crumples up in a process called folding (*centre right*). Many of the Earth's tallest mountain ranges, such as the Himalayas, are "fold mountains" that were created in this way. Folded rocks can be thrust upwards thousands of metres and even fold back on themselves creating an "overfold" (*near right*). When plates move along each other's edges, chunks of land may sink between them, while other chunks called "block mountains" are forced upwards (*far right*).

◀ **The shapes of mountain** ranges change over time. The actions of wind, rain and ice, as well as regular swings in temperature wear away at the rock. Some types of rock wear down more slowly than others, so rounded ridges can become jagged.

Construction and destruction

As molten rock edges its way through gaps between the oceanic plates, it creates and destroys features of the Earth's surface (*see right*). An oceanic ridge builds up along the line where the magma has pushed through, while chains of individual bulges rise up over hot spots where the moving plate passes across a powerful upflow of magma. As the oceanic plate widens, its outer edges may be crumpled up into fold mountains (*see above*) or be forced beneath the edge of the neighbouring continental plate in a process called subduction. The oceanic plate is pushed down into the Earth's mantle where it melts. Some of this melted rock may push its way up again, throwing up chains of islands separated from the fold mountains of the main continent by seas.

◀ **Magma rises from the Earth's mantle** and forces its way between the plates that meet along the ocean floor. This molten rock hardens to form more of the Earth's crust. As is does so, it spreads out from the crack, edging each plate outwards and causing the ocean basin to widen.

North America

- **AREA**
  23,482,844 sq km (9,066,726 sq miles). At its widest point, it extends about 8,000 km (4,960 miles) from the Pacific Ocean to the Atlantic Ocean. Its greatest distance north to south is 6,500 km (3,720 miles) from Alaska in the north to Panama in the south.
- **THIRD-LARGEST CONTINENT**
  North America is the third-largest of the seven continents, covering about one sixth of the total land area of the world.
- **POPULATION**
  Approximately 400 million people. About 7 percent of the world's population lives in North America.
- **LARGEST COUNTRY** (by area)
  Canada, 9,976,140 sq km (3,851,788 sq miles)
- **HIGHEST POINT**
  Denali (Mt McKinley), in Alaska, 6,194 m (20,320 ft) above sea level
- **LOWEST POINT**
  Death Valley, California, 86 m (282 ft) below sea level
- **HIGHEST RECORDED TEMPERATURE**
  57°C (135°F) in Death Valley, California
- **LOWEST RECORDED TEMPERATURE**
  -66°C (-87°F) in Northice, Greenland

▲ **The history of the Earth** comes scarily to life at the San Andreas Fault in California. Two large chunks of the Earth's surface meet along this line in the land. Their constant movement – usually slight – can trigger a series of minor Earth tremors, for which people are prepared. However, serious earthquakes are a constant danger along the fault, especially if the movement is sudden and dramatic. (*See page 15.*)

From your position high above the Isthmus of Panama, the narrow link between North and South America, the land widens out as it stretches northwards. Tropical forests cover North America's short southern border, but the continent has many other landscapes. As we look north, the forests give way to a large, dry area that is bounded to the west by the Rockies, the main mountain range of North America. Rolling eastwards from this dry region are the Great Plains – flat, treeless grasslands extending as far as the lowlands of the mighty Mississippi River. Farther east is the continent's other main range – the Appalachians. Flat lands line the Atlantic coast to the east of this range.

In the far north, beyond a wide band of forests and extending beyond the Arctic Circle, is a vast region where few plants can survive the bitterly cold weather. Hundreds of islands lie along the northern edge of North America, where the continent meets the Arctic Ocean. One of these, Greenland, is one of the largest islands in the world.

▲ **A relatively young mountain range,** the Rockies' jagged peaks have not yet been worn down by the effects of erosion.

① The Rocky Mountains
The Rockies form part of an extremely long chain of mountains that stretches from northernmost North America through Central America and along the western edge of South America, where they become the Andes. (*See also pages 14-15.*)

② The Great Basin
Although the term "basin" usually describes a low-lying valley, the Great Basin of western North America lies on high ground. It is sandwiched between mountain ranges lying to the east and west. Very little rain falls on this rocky region, and the southern edge of the Great Basin is almost a desert. (*See also page 17.*)

▲ **Water and wind carved** away the soft stone of the Monument Valley, through which rivers once ran. Harder rocks resisted the erosion and now tower over the valley.

③ Sonoran Desert
Like most deserts in North America, the Sonoran Desert lies in the narrow strip of land to the west of the Rocky Mountains. It extends from southern Arizona into northern Mexico. The Sonoran Desert is a rugged mixture of mountains and deep valleys. Daytime temperatures soar in the summer but winter nights can be bitterly cold, especially on the higher ground. The Gulf of California separates the Sonoran Desert from Baja California, the long, rocky peninsula, which is almost as dry as the Sonoran Desert itself.

▲ **Joshua trees** are among the few plants that can survive in the dry conditions of the Sonoran Desert. They store enough water in their tough needles to survive long periods without rain.

④ The Grand Canyon
Described as one of the Natural Wonders of the World, the Grand Canyon has been carved out of the land by the waters of the Colorado River. The Grand Canyon is about 446 km (276 miles) long, up to 29 km (18 miles) wide and more than 1,500 m (5,000 ft) deep. Over some 6 million years, the Colorado River has been cutting its way downwards through the canyon, exposing in its steep sides layers of rock and fossils that give information about the Earth's history. The oldest rocks, at the bottom of the canyon, are at least a billion years old. (*See also page 15.*)

⑥ Guiana Highlands and Guyana Shield

Native Americans call the land between the Amazon and Orinoco rivers the "land of waters". The Guiana Highlands (*left*) are covered in thick forests. They receive enormous amounts of rain and supply water to hundreds of streams, which trickle down to meet the larger rivers. To the south of the highlands is a region called the Guyana Shield, a forested plateau that lies on a bed of ancient rock. There are many precious minerals in the soil.

⑦ Amazon Basin

The mighty Amazon River traces its course from the eastern edge of the Andes to the Atlantic Ocean on the other side of the continent. It is not as long as the Nile in Africa, but in some ways it is far greater. More water flows from it than from all eight of the world's next biggest rivers put together! Many hundreds of smaller rivers join it across a huge broad valley, or basin, that is the largest rainforest in the world. (*See also pages 18-19.*)

▲ **The Amazon rainforest** covers about one third of South America. It lies in the Amazon Basin, a land of water and constant high temperatures. These conditions mean that many different types of plants and animals live in the rainforest.

⑧ Pampas

Vast rolling grasslands called the Pampas lie to the east of the Andes in the central part of South America. They stretch as far as the Atlantic Ocean in places. The word pampas is a Native American term meaning "flat surface". The soil in the eastern Pampas is rich and there are many farms. The western Pampas, however, are much drier because the Andes block most of the clouds that would bring rain (*see page 17*).

⑤ Chaco

Sandwiched between the Amazon Basin and the Pampas is a low, flat plain known as the Chaco. Grasslands cover much of the Chaco, but in the west they give way to more forested areas. It is generally hot and dry, but in the summer rainy season (December to April) heavy rains cause its rivers to flood and large parts of the grasslands become swamp.

⑨ Lake Titicaca

The largest lake in South America, Lake Titicaca lies high up in the Andes on a plain known as the Altiplano. Its waters are 3,810 m (12,500 ft) above sea level, making it the highest lake in the world where boats and even small ships can sail. Thick beds of reeds grow along the shores of Lake Titicaca. Native Americans weave these reeds to make boats for use on the lake (*left*).

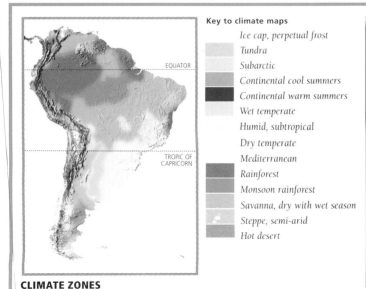

Key to climate maps

- Ice cap, perpetual frost
- Tundra
- Subarctic
- Continental cool summers
- Continental warm summers
- Wet temperate
- Humid, subtropical
- Dry temperate
- Mediterranean
- Rainforest
- Monsoon rainforest
- Savanna, dry with wet season
- Steppe, semi-arid
- Hot desert

CLIMATE ZONES

AVERAGE JANUARY TEMPERATURE

AVERAGE JULY TEMPERATURE

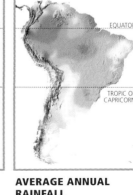

AVERAGE ANNUAL RAINFALL

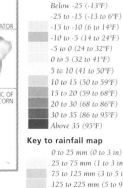

Key to temperature maps °C

- Below -25 (-13°F)
- -25 to -15 (-13 to 6°F)
- -15 to -10 (6 to 14°F)
- -10 to -5 (14 to 24°F)
- -5 to 0 (24 to 32°F)
- 0 to 5 (32 to 41°F)
- 5 to 10 (41 to 50°F)
- 10 to 15 (50 to 59°F)
- 15 to 20 (59 to 68°F)
- 20 to 30 (68 to 86°F)
- 30 to 35 (86 to 95°F)
- Above 35 (95°F)

Key to rainfall map

- 0 to 25 mm (0 to 3 in)
- 25 to 75 mm (1 to 3 in)
- 75 to 125 mm (3 to 5 in)
- 125 to 225 mm (5 to 9 in)
- 225 to 275 mm (9 to 11 in)
- 275 to 375 mm (11 to 15 in)
- 375 to 475 mm (15 to 19 in)
- 475 to 725 mm (19 to 38 in)
- 725 to 975 mm (38 to 58 in)
- 975 to 1,475 mm (38 to 58 in)
- Above 1,475 mm (58 in)

Map labels: Amazon Delta, Araguaia River, Tocantins River, Parnaiba River, Sobradinho Reservoir, São Francisco River, PLATEAU OF BORBOREMA, ...ILIAN SHIELD, Parnaiba River, Rio Grande, BRAZILIAN HIGHLANDS, Iguaçu River, Furnas Reservoir, SERRA GERAL, SERRA DA MANTIQUEIRA, SERRA DO MAR, EQUATOR, TROPIC OF CAPRICORN

Mountains and Valleys

Looking east-southeast from your viewpoint high above Alaska, the western shores of North and South America snake away into the distance. Along the entire stretch, all the way to Cape Horn some 11,000 km (6,820 miles) away, an almost continuous mountain range traces the coastline. We can see the magnificent Rocky Mountains stretching from Alaska down to meet the Sierra Madre mountains in Central America. In the distance are the South American Andes, which contain some of the highest mountains in the world.

HEIGHT OF LAND

	Above 4,000 m (13,000 ft)
	4,000 m (13,000 ft)
	2,000 m (6,500 ft)
	1,500 m (5,000 ft)
	1,000 m (3,200 ft)
	500 m (1,600 ft)
	300 m (1,000 ft)
	150 m (500 ft)
	Sea level

• **NORTH AMERICAN MOUNTAINS**
Highest point: Denali (Mt McKinley), 6,194 m (20,320 ft)
Longest mountain range: the Rocky Mountains, about 3,220 km (2,000 miles) long
Largest glacier: Greenland ice sheet, covering more than 1.8 million sq km (700,000 square miles)

• **SOUTH AMERICAN MOUNTAINS**
Highest point: Aconcagua, 6,960 m (22,834 ft)
Longest mountain range: the Andes, 7,240 km (4,489 miles) long
Highest volcano: Llullaillaco, 6,723 m (22,057 ft)

▲ **The Appalachian Mountains** have the rounded appearance typical of older mountain ranges, which have been worn down by the forces of erosion over many millions of years. Because the mountains are now relatively low – with few summits over 1,830 m (6,000 ft) – they are able to support thick forests all the way up to each peak.

This view is looking east-southeast across the Rockies towards the Caribbean Sea and South America beyond. The map below is how this area is normally shown.

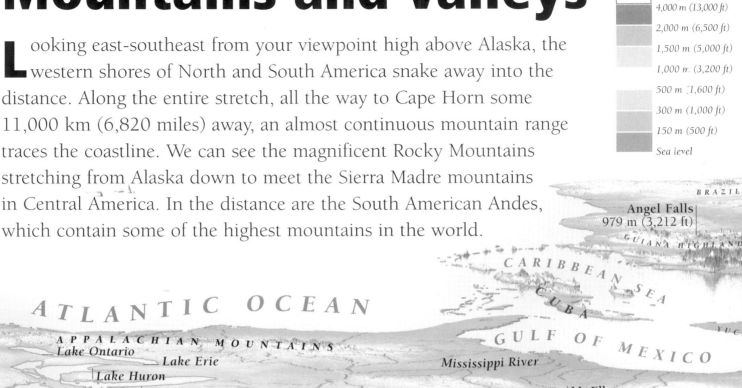

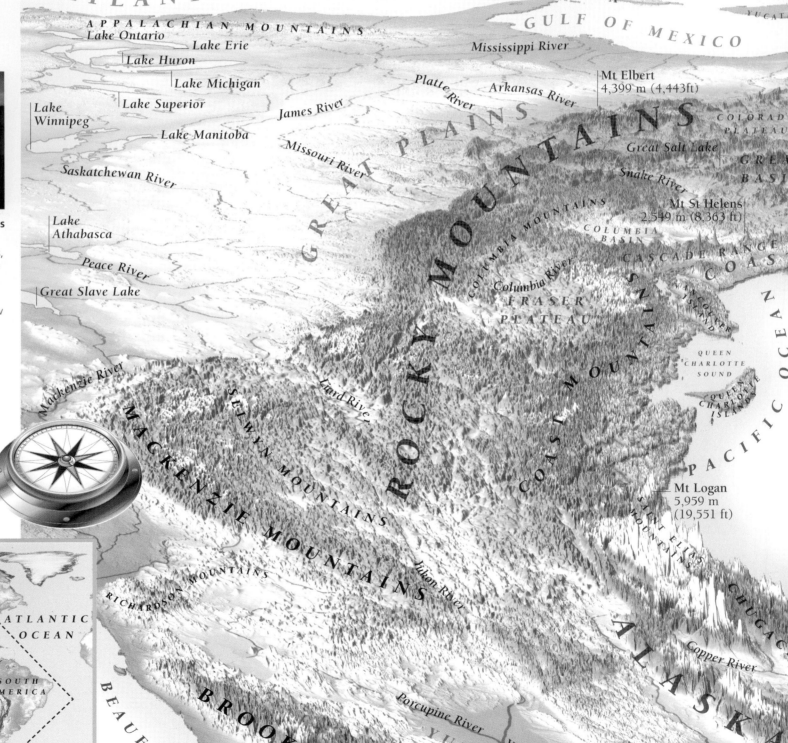

Rising from the Pacific

The movement of the plates below the Pacific Ocean formed both the Andes and the Rocky Mountains about 65 million years ago. The steady pushing of the Nazca Plate into the edge of South America caused the land to crumple up higher and higher, creating the Andes mountains. A similar collision between the Pacific Plate and North America created the Coast Ranges of western North America, although the crumpling was less dramatic. The impact also pushed the North American crust in on itself, forcing the crust upwards farther inland and creating the Rockies. (See also page 7.)

Canyons and gorges

Along its course the Colorado River passes through a dramatic landscape that is its own creation – the Grand Canyon (see page 8). A canyon, also known as a gorge, is a very deep, steep-walled valley, which is often very large. It is usually created high up in a river's course, where the waters are still fast-flowing. The river cuts its way downwards through many layers of rock, leaving a deep valley with its sides exposed as steep cliffs (see right). A waterfall can create a gorge as it cuts its way back up the river's course (see right, inset).

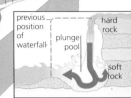

▲ **A waterfall** forms where a river flows over hard rocks onto softer rocks beneath. The softer rocks are pounded away, leaving a steep face over which the water plunges. As the harder rock above crumbles, the position of the waterfall moves upriver.

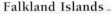

SOUTH AMERICA

Brazilian Highlands

Rising up from the Atlantic coast, about midway down South America, are the Brazilian Highlands, an area of high ground that contains plains, forests and narrow river valleys. Such a large expanse of usually quite level land stretching across high ground is called a plateau – it is also sometimes described as tableland. Most of the Brazilian Highlands lie about 300 to 900 m (1,000 to 3,000 ft) above sea level. Near the coast, however, they rise up sharply in many areas and form steep slopes. The highest peaks, including Pico da Bandeira, 2,890 m (9,482 ft), in the Serra da Mantiqueira, and Pedra Açu, 2,232 m (7,323 ft), are along the southeastern edge of the highlands.

▲ Steep slopes rise up near Nova Friburgo, just 80 km (50 miles) from Brazil's Atlantic coast. This area was once thickly forested, but has become partly deforested as trees have been cleared to make land available for local farming.

San Andreas Fault

The cities of California in North America are sitting on a time bomb, for they lie along the San Andreas Fault. The fault is a giant crack in the Earth's surface – the join between the Pacific and North American plates, two of the huge plates of rock that make up the Earth's rigid shell (see page 7). These plates are always sliding past each other slowly. As they scrape against each other, they set off vibrations all around called tremors. Stronger collisions produce earthquakes, which can cause severe damage. San Francisco was destroyed by an earthquake in 1906 and the Los Angeles suburb of Northridge was badly damaged in 1994. Seismologists, or scientists who study earthquakes, predict that there will be another large earthquake soon.

Earthquakes

The forces at work inside the Earth can break through to the surface as earthquakes along faults between the plates. Earthquakes occur when plates slide past each other or move in the same direction, but at different speeds. Semi-solid rocks in the outer mantle slide against the more brittle rock of the crust, building up pressure. Eventually the brittle rock breaks, sending out shock waves in all directions. This energy causes rocks on the surface to crack and move suddenly, usually along the edge of the fault. If an earthquake occurs beneath the ocean, the shock waves can create a giant wave called a tsunami.

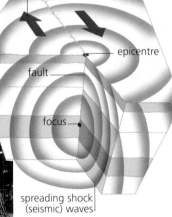

▲ **Oakland, California,** experienced a massive earthquake in October 1989. The force was enough to cause a 2-km (1.2-mile) stretch of elevated freeway to collapse. Oakland and neighbouring San Francisco lie along the San Andreas Fault (see left).

▲ **In an earthquake,** the point where the brittle rock first breaks deep underground is called the focus. The spot on the surface directly above the focus is the epicentre of the earthquake, and damage is usually greatest there. The shock waves, called seismic waves, caused by the initial break in the rock spread out in all directions.

North and South America

ARCTIC CIRCLE
TROPIC OF CANCER
EQUATOR
TROPIC OF CAPRICORN
ANTARCTIC CIRCLE

- **NORTH AMERICAN PLAINS AND DESERTS**

Largest plain: Great Plain, roughly 3.3 million sq km (1.3 million sq miles)

Largest desert: Sonoran Desert, 310,000 sq km (120,000 sq miles)

- **SOUTH AMERICAN PLAINS AND DESERTS**

Largest plain: the Pampas, roughly 2.8 million sq km (1.1 million sq miles)

Largest desert: Patagonia, 777,000 sq km (300,000 sq miles)

World's driest place: Atacama Desert

▲ **The Mojave Desert**, one of the driest regions of North America, occupies much of southeastern California and southern Arizona, and it forms the southern edge of the Great Basin. It has an area of about 38,850 sq km (15,000 sq miles). The Mojave takes its name from a tribe of Native Americans who managed to farm and herd livestock in the harsh conditions.

This view is looking south across central North America. The map below is how this area is normally shown.

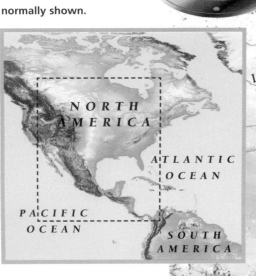

NORTH AMERICA

ATLANTIC OCEAN

PACIFIC OCEAN

SOUTH AMERICA

Plains and Deserts

The Great Plains, which make up most of the "heart" of North America, stretch out before you as you look southwards across the continent from high above northern Canada. They slope gently from west to east, dipping from a height of about 1,200 m (4,000 ft) near the Rocky Mountains down to about 450 m (1,500 ft) as they meet the great valley of the Mississippi and Missouri rivers. This vast area has few trees, although some types of grass and grain can grow in the harsh, dry conditions. West of these lowlands are the Appalachian Mountains, following the east coast of North America almost as far south as the Peninsula of Florida.

▲ **North Dakota**, a US state in the Great Plains, has many farms. Although the region receives little rainfall, it is criss-crossed by many rivers, including the Missouri. This ready source of water enables farmers to irrigate their large fields.

The Great Plains

This immense area of plains, reaching from Canada down to southern Texas, lies on a high plateau that extends eastwards from the Rocky Mountains. The mountains act as a barrier to rain clouds coming in from the Pacific Ocean (*see box opposite*). Tough types of grass can grow naturally along the Great Plains, but farmers have ploughed up vast areas to plant wheat and other grain crops.

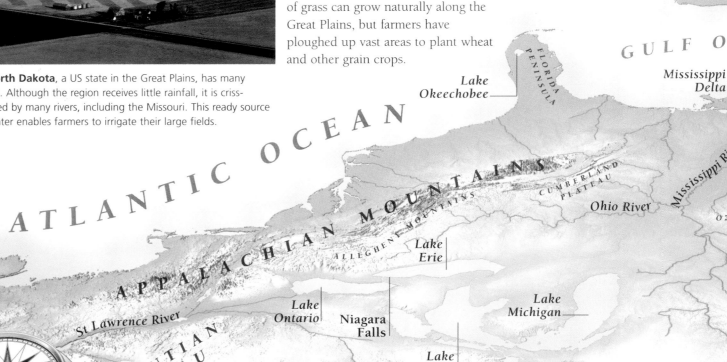

CARIBBEAN SEA

GULF OF HONDURAS

SIERR

YUCATA PENINSU

GULF OF

Mississippi Delta

FLORIDA PENINSULA

Lake Okeechobee

ATLANTIC OCEAN

APPALACHIAN MOUNTAINS

CUMBERLAND PLATEAU

Ohio River

Mississippi River

OZA

ALLEGHENY MOUNTAINS

Lake Erie

Lake Michigan

St Lawrence River

Lake Ontario

Niagara Falls

Lake Huron

LAURENTIAN PLATEAU

Lake Superior

Lake Nipigon

Rupert River

La Grande Rivière

La Grande Rivière de la Baleine

Attawapiskat River

JAMES BAY

Severn River

BELCHER ISLANDS

UNGAVA PENINSULA

OTTAWA ISLANDS

HUDSON BAY

HUDSON STRAIT

MANSEL ISLAND

The Great Basin

Forming a triangle-shaped area of very dry land covering about 543,900 sq km (210,000 sq miles) in western North America, the Great Basin lies between mountain ranges. To the east is the Wasatch Range, while the Sierra Nevada and Cascade ranges rise up to the west, creating a rain shadow (*see box*). A small amount of rain does fall on the Great Basin, but there are very few streams and rivers, and none of them flows into the sea. Instead, they carry water from neighbouring mountains into salty lakes such as Great Salt Lake and Mono Lake. Water in these lakes evaporates in the hot dry air, leaving behind the salts that were dissolved in it, and this makes the remaining water more salty.

◀ **Mono Lake** lies on the eastern side of the Sierra Nevada Mountains. Water from these mountains drains into the lake but can flow no farther. Much of it evaporates.

SOUTH AMERICA

▲ *The Atacama Desert, believed to be the driest place on Earth, lies on a plateau in western South America. The plateau was once even higher than it is today, but it sank after a collision between two of the Earth's plates.*

Rain shadows

Like the Rockies in North America (*see opposite*), the Andes mountains act as a natural barrier to moist air flowing in from the Pacific Ocean to the west of South America. As the moist air from the west is pushed upwards over the mountains, it cools and the moisture turns to rain, which falls on the western slopes. By the time the air has passed over the mountains, there is little or no moisture left for the land lying to the east. The western Pampas, which meet the Andes, lie in this "rain shadow" and receive little moisture. The eastern Pampas, however, are kept well watered by rain from the moist air blowing in from the Atlantic Ocean to the east. In the case of the Atacama, squeezed between two mountain ranges, the loss of rain is nearly complete, creating a desert. A coastal range cuts off rains from the Pacific while the Andes stand in the way of even the slightest bit of rain coming from the east.

As air rises, clouds form, causing rain or snow to fall.

rain clouds

Pacific moist air → dry air → Atlantic moist air

Andes mountains · Patagonia · Coastal Ranges

▲ *Higher land near South America's Atlantic and Pacific coasts forces moist air flowing in from the oceans upwards, causing rain to fall. The clouds are emptied of rain and bring no moisture to the rain shadow lands between.*

▲ *The Pampas are huge treeless plains of central South America. They rise gradually from the Atlantic coast in the east to the Andes mountains in the west. The eastern portion, known as the humid Pampa, is one of the most fertile regions in the continent. Nearer the Andes, this gives way to the dry Pampa, a region that in places is almost as dry as a desert.*

HEIGHT OF LAND

Above 4,000 m (13,000 ft)
4,000 m (13,000 ft)
2,000 m (6,500 ft)
1,500 m (5,000 ft)
1,000 m (3,200 ft)
500 m (1,600 ft)
300 m (1,000 ft)
150 m (500 ft)
Sea level

PACIFIC OCEAN

GULF OF CAMPECHE

MEXICO

Rio Grande

SIERRA MADRE DEL SUR

MEXICAN PLATEAU

SIERRA MADRE OCCIDENTAL

SIERRA MADRE ORIENTAL

BAJA CALIFORNIA

GULF OF CALIFORNIA

SONORAN DESERT

Brazos River

EDWARDS PLATEAU

LLANO ESTACADO

Red River

Arkansas River

COLORADO PLATEAU

Grand Canyon

Colorado River

MOJAVE DESERT

Mt Elbert 4,399 m (14,443 ft)

WASATCH RANGE

GREAT BASIN

ROCKY MOUNTAINS

Missouri River

Platte River

James River

Minnesota River

THE

GREAT PLAINS

Great Salt Lake

Snake River

Lake of the Woods

Yellowstone River

Lake Manitoba

Lake Winnepegosis

South Saskatchewan River

PRAIRES

Lake Winnipeg

North Saskatchewan River

Saskatchewan River

South Indian Lake

Reindeer Lake

Churchill River

Seal River

Lakes and Rivers

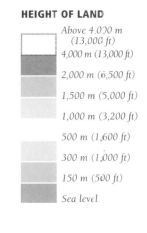

HEIGHT OF LAND

Above 4,000 m (13,000 ft)

4,000 m (13,000 ft)

2,000 m (6,500 ft)

1,500 m (5,000 ft)

1,000 m (3,200 ft)

500 m (1,600 ft)

300 m (1,000 ft)

150 m (500 ft)

Sea level

From high above the Atlantic Ocean, you are looking west-southwest across South America and the mouth of the mighty Amazon River. The Amazon begins its course in the hills near the distant Andes and makes its way across the widest part of the continent, cutting through the vast lowland region of rainforest known as the Amazon Basin. Hundreds of smaller streams and rivers, called tributaries, join the Amazon along its 6,275-km (3,900-mile) course, and together they drain an area of more than 6 million sq km (2.3 million sq miles).

• **NORTH AMERICAN LAKES AND RIVERS**
Longest river: Mississippi, United States, 3,770 km (2,340 miles) long. Mississippi-Missouri River system, 5,970 km (3,710 miles)
Largest lake: Lake Superior, 82,100 sq km (31,700 sq miles)

• **SOUTH AMERICAN LAKES AND RIVERS**
Longest river: Amazon River, Brazil, 6,275 km (3,900 miles)
Largest lake: Lake Titicaca, Peru/Bolivia, 8,192 sq km (3,200 sq miles)
World's highest waterfall: Angel Falls, 979 m (3,212 ft)

The Amazon River and its delta

Although the Amazon is the second-longest river in the world after the Nile, it is the largest river in several ways. No other river has as many tributaries as the Amazon. Depending on whether it is the dry or wet season, the Amazon empties into the Atlantic Ocean between 34 million and 121 million litres (7.2 million and 26 million gallons) of water each second. Overall, this enormous volume accounts for one-fifth of all the fresh water that drains into the oceans of the world. And with this water is a great deal of soil and sediment that has been carried along by the river. Each day, the Amazon dumps millions of tons of sediment near its mouth. The immense volume of water and sediment is so great that it changes the colour of the Atlantic Ocean over a huge distance.

Lake Titicaca is fed by many small streams that run down from the slopes of the Andes mountains. At its deepest the lake is 475 m (174 ft), and it has an average width of 56 km (35 miles). South America has very few large lakes, but most of them – like Titicaca – lie in valleys high up in the Andes.

This view across the Amazon Basin is looking west-southwest towards the Andes and the Pacific Ocean beyond. The map below is how this area is normally shown.

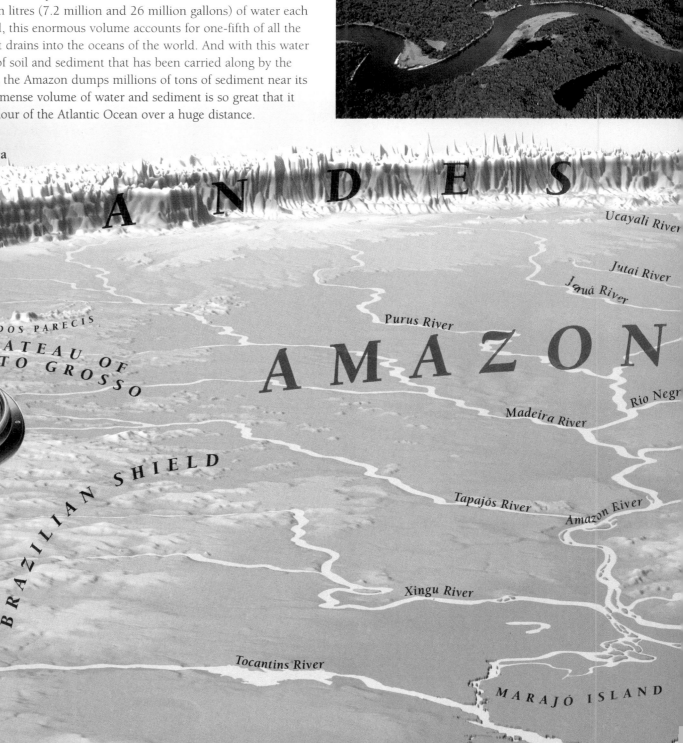

Lake Titicaca

ANDES

Ucayali River

Jutai River

Jauá River

Purus River

SERRA DOS PARECIS
PLATEAU OF MATTO GROSSO

AMAZON

Madeira River

Rio Negro

BRAZILIAN SHIELD

Tapajós River

Amazon River

Xingu River

Tocantins River

MARAJÓ ISLAND

ATLANTIC OCEAN

SOUTH AMERICA

PACIFIC OCEAN

Mississippi-Missouri River System

Flowing through a vast, low-lying region in central North America are the Mississippi and Missouri rivers. They drain the whole area that lies between the Rocky Mountains in the west and the Appalachians in the east. Near their sources, these rivers follow the channels created when melting water from retreating glaciers cut through the soft soil about 10,000 years ago. Each river widens and slows down as it flows south. Their confluence, or meeting point, is near the city of St Louis in the heart of North America. Together, they are often known as the Mississippi-Missouri River System, which is one of the largest waterway systems in the world.

► *Along its lower stretch, the Mississippi River passes through a low-lying plain, laced with smaller tributaries, lakes and ponds. Forests of trees thrive in the region, thanks to the rich soil that the river constantly deposits.*

◄ **A lush landscape** surrounds much of the Amazon River. Here, about midway along its course, dense forests stretch away into the distance, with several of the many tributaries that join the Amazon also visible.

▲ **A satellite photograph** of the mouth of the Amazon shows how much silt the river carries. About 3 million tonnes of sediment is released into the Atlantic Ocean each day, causing the seawater to appear green as far as 320 km (200 miles) from the nearest land.

Oxbow lakes

As a river moves down its valley and onto flatter land, it flows more slowly and its course starts to wander from side to side, forming loops, called meanders. Sometimes, the river cuts through the neck of one of its loops, making a "short cut" and straightening the course of the river again. The old loop is left cut off as an oxbow lake. Its name comes from the lake's shape, which is like the U-shaped collar (or oxbow) worn by oxen for pulling a plough or wagon. There are many oxbow lakes along the slow-moving stretch of the Mississippi River as it nears the Gulf of Mexico.

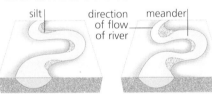

silt   direction of flow of river   meander   oxbow lake

1 Silt builds up where the flow of water is slowest, creating a loop in the river.

2 The river cuts into the loop, called a meander, as it deposits more silt.

3 Eventually, the river cuts through the loop, isolating the meander as an oxbow lake.

Great Lakes

The five Great Lakes of North America contain about one-fifth of all the world's fresh water. Lake Superior, the largest, contains 12,100 cubic km (2,900 cubic miles) of water – more than the other four Great Lakes combined. The amount of water in a lake depends on its surface area but also on its average depth. Lake Erie has the fourth-largest surface area, but contains the least water because it is relatively shallow – it has an average depth of only 19 m (62 ft).

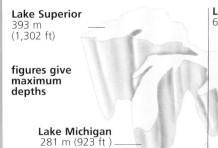

Lake Superior
393 m
(1,302 ft)

Lake Erie
64 m (210 ft)

Lake Huron
229 m (750 ft)

figures give maximum depths

Lake Ontario
237 m (778 ft)

Lake Michigan
281 m (923 ft)

PACIFIC OCEAN

GALAPAGOS ISLANDS

CORDILLERA REAL

Napo River

Amazon River

Içá River

Japurá River

BASIN

GUIANA HIGHLANDS

Branco River

Mapuera River

Rio Paru de Oeste

GUYANA SHIELD

Paru River

AMAZON DELTA

ATLANTIC OCEAN

- **AREA**
  10,400,000 sq km (4,000,00 sq miles). It extends about 5,200 km (3,225 miles) from the Atlantic Ocean in the west to the Ural Mountains in the east, between the Mediterranean Sea and the Arctic Ocean.
- **SIXTH-LARGEST CONTINENT**
  Europe is the sixth-largest continent of the world, covering roughly 7 percent of the world's land area. Only Australia is smaller than Europe.
- **POPULATION**
  Approximately 710 milion, which is 12 percent of the population of the world.
- **LARGEST COUNTRY** (by area)
  The European part of the Russian Federation, 3,955,818 sq km (1,527,349 sq miles)
- **HIGHEST POINT**
  Mt Elbrus, in the Russian Federation, 5,642 m (18,510 ft) above sea level
- **LOWEST POINT**
  Caspian Sea, in the Russian Federation, 28 m (92 ft) below sea level
- **HIGHEST RECORDED TEMPERATURE**
  50°C (122°F) in Seville, Spain
- **LOWEST RECORDED TEMPERATURE**
  -55°C (-67°F) in Ust' Shchugor, Russian Federation

▲ **The Atlantic Ocean** continues to play a huge role in forming the landscape of much of its coastline. Along many stretches of Britain's coast, the constant action of the ocean's tides and currents eats away at the soft stone, causing land to fall away into the sea. Rich, fertile meadows often end suddenly as steep cliffs at the point where the sea has eaten away at the shore, such as here at Beachy Head in southern England.

Europe

As you look north over the Mediterranean Sea, you first notice Europe's great east-west expanse. The continent extends more than 5,200 km (3,225 miles) from the slopes of the Ural Mountains in the east to the shores of the Atlantic Ocean in the west. Southern Europe, bordering the Mediterranean, is mainly mountainous and dry. Great mountain ranges, including the Pyrenees, Alps and Balkans, separate this southern region from the rest of the continent. Forests and plains stretch across nearly the whole length of northern Europe. Farther north still is Scandinavia, a land of many lakes and deep coastal valleys. Northernmost Europe lies north of the Arctic Circle. Few trees grow there and the soil is frozen for much of the year. The European islands of Great Britain, Ireland and Iceland lie in the Atlantic Ocean – each has a landscape and climate that has been shaped by damp ocean winds.

ICELAND
① *VATNAJÖK*

◀ **Geysers** are jets of hot steam and water, forced up through cracks in the ground by the heat of volcanic activity. There are many geysers on Iceland.

① Iceland
The island of Iceland lies in the Atlantic Ocean about 1,240 miles (2,000 km) from the European mainland. It is a relatively young island, formed by movement of the Earth's plates about 2 million years ago. Gaps appeared between the plates, creating vents through which lava and gas escape. The cooling lava gradually built up to form the island, which is still being shaped by the volcanic activity beneath.

◀ **The Dolomites** are a mountain range in northern Italy that forms part of the Alps. Many of the needlelike peaks are made of a mineral called dolomite, which has a rosy-pink colour.

② The Alps
Rising up from the heart of Europe are the Alps, a great mountain range that blocks the warm Mediterranean air from reaching northern Europe. Many of the Alpine peaks are distinctively pointed, including the tallest peak, Mont Blanc, which is 4,807 m (15,771 ft) high. Many of Europe's rivers begin their course in the Alps. These fast-flowing rivers often follow paths created by glaciers during the ice ages, forming steep-sided valleys in the mountains.

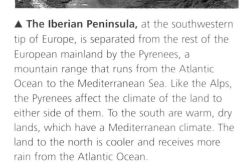

▲ **The Iberian Peninsula,** at the southwestern tip of Europe, is separated from the rest of the European mainland by the Pyrenees, a mountain range that runs from the Atlantic Ocean to the Mediterranean Sea. Like the Alps, the Pyrenees affect the climate of the land to either side of them. To the south are warm, dry lands, which have a Mediterranean climate. The land to the north is cooler and receives more rain from the Atlantic Ocean.

ATLANTIC OCEAN

Duero River
M
Tagus River
IBERIAN

③ Spanish tablelands
Most of the land in the interior of the Iberian Peninsula is a huge, dry plain known as a tableland, or *meseta* in Spanish. The plain (*pictured right*) is a high plateau, which means that winters can be very cold because temperatures drop as land rises from sea level. In summer, however, temperatures are scorching because warm winds sweep in from Africa. With few clouds in the sky, the fierce sun beats down and dries up the landscape.

Africa

- **AREA**
  About 30,097,000 sq km
  (11,620,451 sq miles).
  It extends about 6,760 km
  (4,200 miles) from the
  Mediterranean Sea in the north
  to its southern tip at the Cape
  of Good Hope. It lies between
  the Atlantic and Indian oceans,
  reaching a maximum width of
  about 4,800 km (3,000 miles)
  just south of the Sahara Desert.
- **SECOND-LARGEST CONTINENT**
  Africa is the second-largest
  continent of the world,
  covering roughly 20 percent of
  the world's land area. Only
  Asia is larger than Africa.
- **POPULATION**
  Approximately 750 million
  which is 12.5 percent of the
  population of the world.
- **LARGEST COUNTRY** (by area)
  Sudan, 967,493 sq miles
  (2,505,810 sq km)
- **HIGHEST POINT**
  Mt Kilimanjaro,
  in Tanzania, 5,895 m
  (19,340 ft) above sea level
- **LOWEST POINT**
  Lake Assal, in Djibouti, 156 m
  (512 ft) below sea level
- **HIGHEST RECORDED TEMPERATURE**
  58°C (136°F) in Al 'Aziziyah,
  Libya
- **LOWEST RECORDED TEMPERATURE**
  -24°C (-11°F) in Ilfrane,
  Morocco

▲ **The Congo River** threads its
way through Central Africa like
a giant, upside-down "U".
Along most of its course the
river passes either side of the
equator, through a region of
Africa that receives heavy rainfall
throughout the year. These hot,
humid conditions have helped
to create the second-largest
rainforest in the world. Only the
Amazon rainforest in South
America is larger.

Looking northwest over the Indian Ocean you can see how large Africa is. Much of the continent is very dry or even desert, including the lands to either side of the Nile River. Stretching to the west of there and northwards to the Mediterranean Sea is the Sahara, the largest desert in the world. South of these dry regions are very different landscapes – dense rainforest in the Congo Basin and vast grasslands known as savanna extending east and south from the Basin. Running down through the whole eastern side of the continent is the Great Rift Valley, with mountains and lakes on either side. At the very southern end of Africa are more highlands and dry regions. Madagascar, the world's fourth-largest island, lies to the east in the Indian Ocean.

① Sahara Desert

The vast Sahara Desert covers nearly all of the northern third of Africa. It stretches from the Atlantic Ocean eastward to the Red Sea. Although all of the Sahara is very dry – and some areas see no rain for years – it includes many different landscapes. There are huge regions of sandy dunes (*pictured right*), rocky plains and mountains. The only places where plants grow easily are the small areas known as oases, which receive water from underground (*see pages 29 and 42*).

② Kalahari Desert and Okavango Delta

Extending across a large area of southwest Africa is the Kalahari Desert. It is a rocky region, with many hills and valleys, where shrubs and some grasses survive the heat and lack of water. To the east the Kalahari becomes sandier, with many dunes created by the wind. The Okavango River flows southwards towards the Kalahari but empties into the dry plains to the north of the desert. There the river forms a marshy delta made up of countless channels and many islands. During the winter rainy season, the water level rises and the delta becomes larger, allowing a greater variety of plant life to flourish.

▼ **Only low-growing scrub** and grasses can survive throughout most of the Kalahari Desert. The vegetation must be hardy enough to withstand the area's long periods without rain.

NAMIB
Orange River
GREAT KAROO
Cape of
Good Hope

◀ **A tributary** breaks up into a maze of meanders as it enters the Okavango Delta. For more than 2 million years, silt carried by the Okavango and other rivers has been deposited on the flat terrain, improving the quality of the soil.

▶ **The Nile River** provides an important transportation route and is an essential source of water for most of Egypt's population.

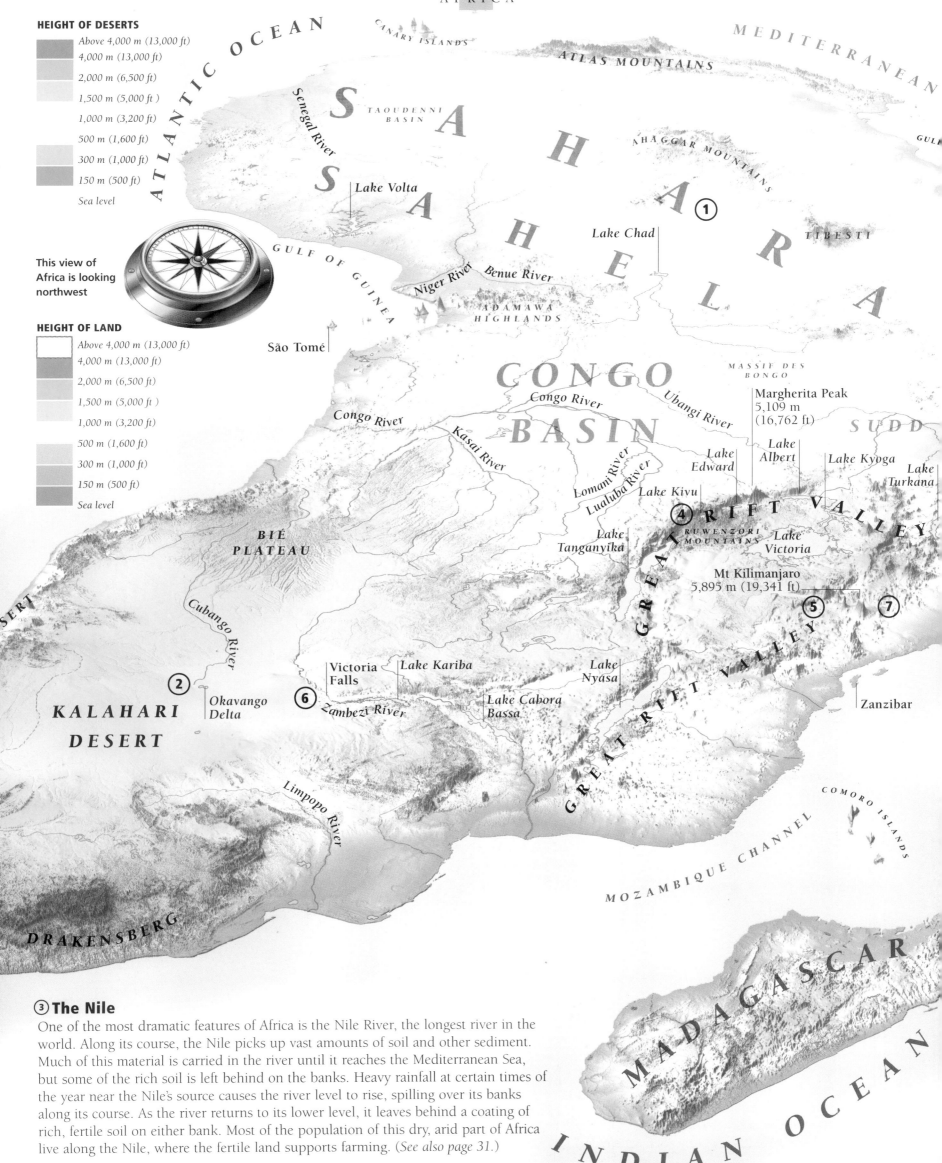

HEIGHT OF DESERTS

Above 4,000 m (13,000 ft)
4,000 m (13,000 ft)
2,000 m (6,500 ft)
1,500 m (5,000 ft)
1,000 m (3,200 ft)
500 m (1,600 ft)
300 m (1,000 ft)
150 m (500 ft)

Sea level

This view of
Africa is looking
northwest

HEIGHT OF LAND

Above 4,000 m (13,000 ft)
4,000 m (13,000 ft)
2,000 m (6,500 ft)
1,500 m (5,000 ft)
1,000 m (3,200 ft)
500 m (1,600 ft)
300 m (1,000 ft)
150 m (500 ft)

Sea level

ATLANTIC OCEAN

CANARY ISLANDS

MEDITERRANEAN

ATLAS MOUNTAINS

SAHARA

SAHEL

TAOUDENNI BASIN

AHAGGAR MOUNTAINS

TIBESTI

GUL

Senegal River

Lake Volta

①

Lake Chad

GULF OF GUINEA

Niger River

Benue River

ADAMAWA HIGHLANDS

MASSIF DES BONGO

SUDD

São Tomé

CONGO BASIN

Congo River

Congo River

Ubangi River

Margherita Peak
5,109 m
(16,762 ft)

Kasai River

Lomani River

Lualuba River

Lake Kivu

Lake Edward

Lake Albert

Lake Kyoga

Lake Turkana

④ GREAT RIFT VALLEY

RUWENZORI MOUNTAINS

Lake Tanganyika

Lake Victoria

Mt Kilimanjaro
5,895 m (19,341 ft)

⑤

⑦

BIÉ PLATEAU

Cubango River

Victoria Falls

Lake Kariba

Lake Nyasa

Lake Cabora Bassa

GREAT RIFT VALLEY

Zanzibar

②

⑥

Okavango Delta

Zambezi River

KALAHARI DESERT

DESERT

Limpopo River

COMORO ISLANDS

DRAKENSBERG

MOZAMBIQUE CHANNEL

MADAGASCAR

③ The Nile

One of the most dramatic features of Africa is the Nile River, the longest river in the world. Along its course, the Nile picks up vast amounts of soil and other sediment. Much of this material is carried in the river until it reaches the Mediterranean Sea, but some of the rich soil is left behind on the banks. Heavy rainfall at certain times of the year near the Nile's source causes the river level to rise, spilling over its banks along its course. As the river returns to its lower level, it leaves behind a coating of rich, fertile soil on either bank. Most of the population of this dry, arid part of Africa live along the Nile, where the fertile land supports farming. (*See also page 31.*)

INDIAN OCEAN

④ The Ruwenzori

Along the western edge of the Great Rift Valley in Central Africa lie the Ruwenzori Mountains. Like the valley, these former volcanoes were formed by violent action below the Earth's crust. Their snow-capped peaks, towering over the hot plains, led European explorers of the 19th century to call them the Mountains of the Moon. The highest peak is Margherita Peak, which reaches to 5,109 m (16,762 ft). The mountains have a wealth of plant life.

▲ **Lobelias** and other flowering plants grow to enormous heights in the Ruwenzori Range because of the rich volcanic soil and ample rainfall.

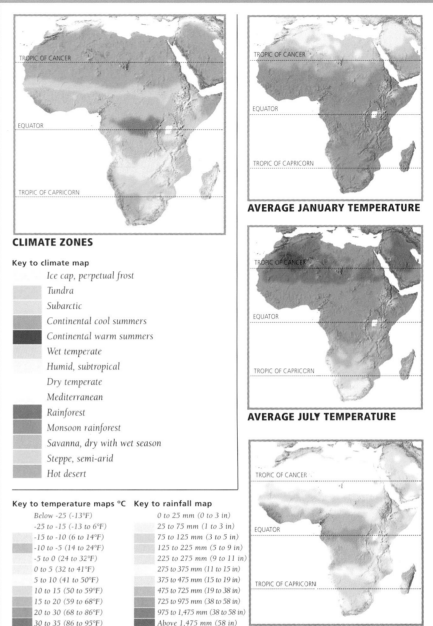

CLIMATE ZONES

Key to climate map

- Ice cap, perpetual frost
- Tundra
- Subarctic
- Continental cool summers
- Continental warm summers
- Wet temperate
- Humid, subtropical
- Dry temperate
- Mediterranean
- Rainforest
- Monsoon rainforest
- Savanna, dry with wet season
- Steppe, semi-arid
- Hot desert

AVERAGE JANUARY TEMPERATURE

AVERAGE JULY TEMPERATURE

AVERAGE ANNUAL RAINFALL

Key to temperature maps °C	Key to rainfall map
Below -25 (-13°F)	0 to 25 mm (0 to 3 in)
-25 to -15 (-13 to 6°F)	25 to 75 mm (1 to 3 in)
-15 to -10 (6 to 14°F)	75 to 125 mm (3 to 5 in)
-10 to -5 (14 to 24°F)	125 to 225 mm (5 to 9 in)
-5 to 0 (24 to 32°F)	225 to 275 mm (9 to 11 in)
0 to 5 (32 to 41°F)	275 to 375 mm (11 to 15 in)
5 to 10 (41 to 50°F)	375 to 475 mm (15 to 19 in)
10 to 15 (50 to 59°F)	475 to 725 mm (19 to 38 in)
15 to 20 (59 to 68°F)	725 to 975 mm (38 to 58 in)
20 to 30 (68 to 86°F)	975 to 1,475 mm (38 to 58 in)
30 to 35 (86 to 95°F)	Above 1,475 mm (58 in)
Above 35 (95°F)	

⑤ Great Rift Valley

Stretching northwards across much of East Africa, then across the Red Sea and into southwestern Asia, is the Great Rift Valley. Steep sides rise as high as 2,000 m (6,562 ft) from the valley floor along much of its length. In most places the valley is between 30 km (19 miles) and 100 km (62 miles) wide. Alongside it are Africa's largest lakes as well as mountain ranges containing the continent's highest peaks. The valley and its neighbouring lakes and mountains were all created millions of years ago by powerful forces below the Earth's surface (*see page 26*).

⑥ Victoria Falls

One of the world's most magnificent waterfalls, Victoria Falls (*right*) is formed as the Zambezi River plunges 108 m (354 ft) from a flat plain into a narrow gorge. It then rushes through the 122-m (400-ft) deep gorge for the next 72 km (45 miles). Over the first 805 km (500 miles) of its journey from its source in northwestern Zambia, the Zambezi River falls only about 183 km (600 ft). Its flow and volume increase, however, about 98 km (60 miles) above Victoria Falls, when it meets the Linyanti River. The Zambezi is about 1.6 km (1 mile) wide before the falls, and it carries an enormous amount of water. The constant mist and noise of the waterfall accounts for its local name, Mosi-oa-Tunya, or "smoke that thunders".

▲ **Herds of animals,** such as these zebra, graze in the forests that reach up to the lower slopes of snow-capped Mt Kilimanjaro.

⑦ Mt Kilimanjaro

Rising up to the east of the Great Rift Valley is Mt Kilimanjaro, the highest mountain in Africa. This temporarily inactive (or dormant) volcano is made up of two peaks, which stand about 11 km (7 miles) apart. Kibo, the higher peak, is 5,895 m (19,340 ft) above sea level, and the peak of Mawensi is 5,149 m (16,892 ft). Air becomes colder the higher it is so, although Kilimanjaro lies very near the equator, its taller peak is covered with snow throughout the year.

Map labels: SEA, OF SIRTE, LIBYAN DESERT, QUATTARA DEPRESSION, Nile Delta, ③, Lake Nasser, NUBIAN DESERT, RED SEA, White Nile, Blue Nile, Lake Tana, ETHIOPIAN HIGHLANDS, GREAT RIFT VALLEY, GULF OF ADEN, Lake Assal, Juba River, Shebeli River, HORN OF AFRICA, TROPIC OF CANCER, EQUATOR, TROPIC OF CAPRICORN

Mountains and Valleys

Above 4,000 m (13,000 ft)
4,000 m (13,000 ft)
2,000 m (6,500 ft)
1,500 m (5,000 ft)
1,000 m (3,200 ft)
500 m (1,600 ft)
300 m (1,000 ft)
150 m (500 ft)
Sea level

Looking roughly southwest towards the familiar "boot" shape of Italy, you can see beneath you the great curve of the Alps, one of the main mountain ranges in Europe. The Alps were formed when two of the Earth's plates pushed together, causing the land to "fold" upwards (*see page 7*) into a series of steep mountains. Mostly during the ice ages, huge sheets of ice, called glaciers, changed the way these mountains looked. The slow-moving glaciers pushed between the mountains, carving out valleys as they went. There are still glaciers in the Alps, and they continue to change the landscape.

• **EUROPEAN MOUNTAINS AND VALLEYS**
Highest point: Mt Elbrus, in the Caucasus Mountains, 5,642 m (18,510 ft).
Glaciers: 2 percent of the Alps are covered by glaciers.

• **AFRICAN MOUNTAINS AND VALLEYS**
Highest point: Mt Kilimanjaro, 5,895 m (19,341 ft).
Glaciers: There are no glaciers in Africa. Even during the ice ages, only a small area around Mt Kilimanjaro was covered by glaciers.

SICILY

Mt Etna
3,340 m (10,958 ft)

TYRRHENIAN SEA

IONIAN SEA

Vesuvius
1,277 m (4,190 ft)

GULF OF TARANTO

LE MURGE

A P E N

Corno Grande
2,914 m (9,560 ft)

The Burren (*above*) is a hilly region of limestone in western Ireland. Its surface has been eroded so much that it is completely bare, except for a few tiny plants that grow in cracks in the limestone. Below ground level is a series of caves formed by water carving its way through the soft limestone (*see also page 41*). Sometimes the roof of a cave collapses so that it opens to the ground above.

This view across the Alps is looking west-southwest over Italy and the Mediterranean Sea. The map below is how this area is normally shown.

AFRICA

The Great Rift Valley

This feature lies on a 50-million-year-old zone of weakness in the Earth's crust, which shows up as a huge fault. The edge of the plate on which Africa lies pushed upwards, causing the Earth's crust to split apart along this fault (**1**). The blocks of crust in the middle of the gap slipped downwards, leaving a steep ridge on either side (**2**). This process continued for millions of years, each time causing more blocks of crust to sink down and creating new ridges (**3**). Some of the most dramatic effects took place about 3.5 million years ago, when volcanoes also formed along the side of the valley.

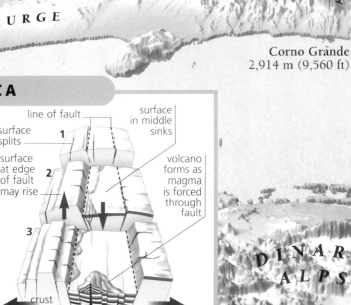

line of fault
surface splits
surface in middle sinks
surface at edge of fault may rise
volcano forms as magma is forced through fault
crust stretches
rising magma

DINARIC ALPS

GREAT HUNGARIAN PLAIN

Sava River

Drava River

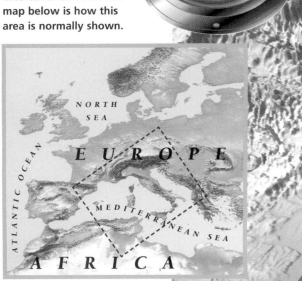

NORTH SEA

EUROPE

ATLANTIC OCEAN

MEDITERRANEAN SEA

AFRICA

▲ *Mt Longonot was once an active volcano. The same forces that created the Great Rift Valley pushed lava up through openings in the Earth's surface, forming volcanoes.*

▶ *The Great Rift Valley (shown here in dark green) extends more than 4,830 km (3,000 miles) from southwestern Asia to southeastern Africa. Its width ranges from a few kilometres to more than 160 km (100 miles). In eastern Africa the valley separates into two branches: the Eastern Rift and the Western Rift.*

Landscapes left behind

Distinctive features remain on the valley landscape long after the glacier has melted. If more than one cirque meet, the mountain between them is often carved into a pyramidal, or pyramid-shaped, peak. Water remaining at the base of a cirque forms a mountain lake, or tarn. Waterfalls pour out of the valleys carved by tributary glaciers, which can be left "hanging" on the steep side of the main valley. Sand and gravel may be left behind along the valley floor in snakelike ridges called eskers or long, rounded hills called drumlins. At the base of the valley are erratics, large rocks deposited by glaciers, as well as small depressions called kettles, where chunks of ice have broken off and melted.

▲ **As a glacier creeps** downwards its incredible power carves the landscape. The lower end of the Stein-gletscher glacier in the Swiss Alps (*pictured here*) has melted to form a meltwater lake.

Glaciers

Snow falling high up in mountains can build up layer upon layer, with the weight of each new layer pushing down upon the ones below. The weight turns the snow to ice, forming a river of ice, or glacier, which moves slowly downhill. Fragments of rock broken from the sides of the valley by the ice line the edge of the glacier, forming lateral moraines. When a glacier meets a smaller, or tributary, glacier the lateral moraines join, forming a medial moraine in the middle of the larger glacier. The ice melts at the lower end of a glacier, and the ground moraine that has been ploughed up beneath the glacier is deposited as a terminal moraine.

top of glacier worn into bowl shape, or cirque
medial moraine
tributary glacier
meltwater lake
ground moraine
lateral moraine
terminal moraine
crevasses (cracks along the surface)

U-shaped valley with wide, flat bottom carved by glacier
esker
hanging valley with waterfall
terminal moraine
tarn
pyramidal peak
kettle
drumlins and erratics

PYRENEES
MASSIF CENTRAL
Rhône River
MARITIME ALPS
Mont Blanc
4,807 m (15,771 ft)
Saône River
Lake Geneva
Matterhorn
4,478 m (14,692 ft)
BERNESE ALPS
JURA MTS
Lake Neuchâtel
GULF OF GENOA
APENNINES
Po River
Lake Garda
PO RIVER BASIN
Rhine River
Adige River
BLACK FOREST
ADRIATIC SEA
DOLOMITES
THE ALPS
Lake Constance
GULF OF VENICE
BAVARIAN ALPS
KITZBÜHLER ALPEN
Brenner Pass
Grossglockner
3,797 m (12,457 ft)
CENTRAL GERMAN UPLANDS
Drau River
Salzach River
Mura River
Inn River
Isar River
Danube River
Danube River
BOHEMIAN FOREST

Plains and Deserts

As you look southwards from high above the Mediterranean Sea, you see the vast, dry expanse of the Sahara Desert reaching deep into Africa – it takes up about one third of the whole of the continent. The Sahara is about 1,610 km (1,000 miles) wide and about 5,150 km (3,200 miles) long from east to west. Overall, it covers more than 9 million sq km (3.5 million sq miles). The Sahara was once a fertile area, but drier weather conditions turned the land into the arid landscape of today. To the south is the semi-desert region known as the Sahel and, in the distance, near the southern tip of Africa, are two more desert regions – the Namib and the Kalahari. Taking up much of eastern Africa are the expanses of savanna, stretching east and south from the Congo Basin.

- **EUROPEAN PLAINS AND DESERTS**
Largest plain: North European Plain, about 2.4 million sq km (950,000 sq miles)
Largest desert: there are no deserts in Europe

- **AFRICAN PLAINS AND DESERTS**
Largest plain: (with clear borders) Serengeti, 14,760 sq km (5,700 sq miles)
World's largest desert: Sahara Desert, about 9 million sq km (3.5 million sq miles)

The Sahel is a dry grassland area that lies between the Sahara Desert to the north and the wetter, tropical regions to the south. Shrubs and some hardy grasses grow there, watered by the small amount of rain that falls mainly between June and September. A few trees grow, but as people cut these down for firewood, the soil becomes loosened and blows away. This process allows the Sahara to advance, covering the edge of the Sahel with sand. In this way, the Sahel is shrinking as the Sahara grows bigger.

This view across Africa is looking south-southwest over the Sahara towards the Atlantic Ocean. The map below is how this area is normally shown.

▲ **With so few trees** on the African savanna, the tall, steep-sided outcrops of rock known as kopjes are clear landmarks. Kopjes are blocks of bedrock – the layer of solid rock that lies beneath the soil – that have been forced upwards and now stand about 10 m (33 feet) above the grassland floor.

The savanna

The African savanna, one of the world's great grassland plains (*see box on page 29*), is a delicately balanced natural landscape. The amount of rainfall determines what type of plants will thrive along with the tough grasses that can grow in very dry conditions. More rain means more trees, but animals also play a part in controlling the landscape. Large animals, such as elephants and rhinos, eat the tree branches and allow the grasses to take over again. Intensive grazing by wildebeests, gazelles and other animals also helps the grass. The constant "mowing" prevents species of long grass from taking over. As herds graze, their saliva encourages the grass to grow more, and when they move on, they leave behind nutrient-rich urine and dung.

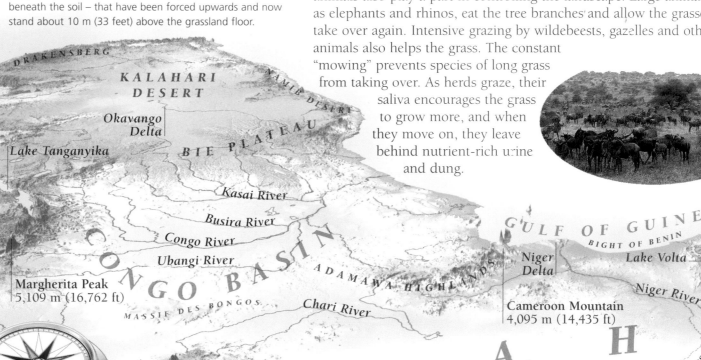

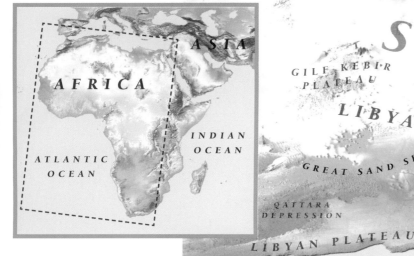

Types of dune

Several different types of dune form in sandy deserts like many areas of the Sahara. The difference between these dunes lies in their shape, which is formed by the wind as it blows the tiny grains of sand into heaps. Dunes grow in height as well as along the ground and may travel as much as 30 m (100 ft) in a year. No matter what shape the dune becomes, the side facing the wind is always longer and less steep than the side facing away.

A barchan dune has a crescent-shaped front where the sand has built up higher. The ends of the crescent are lower and so are more easily blown along, forming two long tails. Barchan dunes often form in a long series.

Seif dunes form where the wind has changed direction and has dragged out the tails of barchan dunes until they merge.

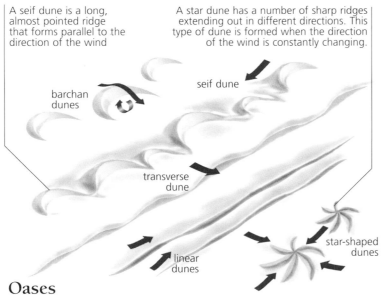

A seif dune is a long, almost pointed ridge that forms parallel to the direction of the wind

A star dune has a number of sharp ridges extending out in different directions. This type of dune is formed when the direction of the wind is constantly changing.

barchan dunes

seif dune

transverse dune

linear dunes

star-shaped dunes

Constant steady winds produce a linear dune, which cuts a trough in the desert floor. The sand then piles up in dunes that look like long, rounded fingers from the air.

Oases

Water running off mountains often travels a long way underground and may collect in an aquifer – an area of rock that can hold water but lies between other types of rock that will not allow water through. If there is a fault, or crack, in the rock above the aquifer, the water is often forced up to the surface. In the middle of a dry desert such a well-watered area can be very fertile, allowing plants to grow and creating an oasis. (See also page 42.)

(See also page 42.)

▶ **Date palms** form a thick grove around this oasis in the Sahara. Plants can grow in these dry surroundings because of the steady supply of water from underground.

HEIGHT OF DESERTS

4,000 m (13,000 ft)
2,000 m (6,500 ft)
1,500 m (5,000 ft)
1,000 m (3,200 ft)
500 m (1,600 ft)
300 m (1,000 ft)
150 m (500 ft)
Sea level

HEIGHT OF LAND

Above 4,000 m (13,000 ft)
4,000 m (13,000 ft)
2,000 m (6,500 ft)
1,500 m (5,000 ft)
1,000 m (3,200 ft)
500 m (1,600 ft)
300 m (1,000 ft)
150 m (500 ft)
Sea level

ATLANTIC OCEAN

Gambia River
Senegal River

TAOUDENNI BASIN

PLATEAU DU TADEMAIT

ERG CHECH

ERG IGUIDI

CANARY ISLANDS

GRAND ERG OCCIDENTAL

ORIENTAL

ATLAS MOUNTAINS

Jbel Toubkal
4,165 m (13,365 ft)

Jbel Avachi
3,737 m (12,257 ft)

Strait of Gibraltar

IBERIAN PENINSULA

BALEARIC ISLANDS

▲ Unlike in other parts of the world where layers of sedimentary rock have been thrust upwards to form towering mountains, the plains that stretch across northern Europe have remained flat.

The Steppe

Spreading across much of southwest Russia and east into western Asia is a vast grassland region known as the Steppe. These grasslands mark the eastern edge of the North European Plain (see page 22), which lies on a bed of sedimentary rock, formed from parts of dead plants and animals and fragments of old, worn-down rock that settled together millions of years ago. Glaciers from the ice ages scraped the surface of the land level and left behind the soil that had been ploughed up along the way.

Some of the best soils of Europe are found on the North European Plain, particularly along its southern margin, where winds deposit a fine, fertile material called loess. The loess contains minerals important for plant life and can help water drain through the soil. The Steppe in the east of the Plain have an extreme continental climate, with hot, dry summers and cold, snowy winters. In these harsh conditions, few trees grow but the rich soil enables farmers to raise many crops.

▶ The rich soil of the Steppe is known as chernozem, which means "dark earth" in Russian. This type of soil runs deep into the ground and, as its name suggests, has a dark colour. Chernozem contains a large amount of humus (partly decayed plant and animal matter) and is rich in lime and other minerals that increase soil fertility.

Grasslands

The European Steppe and the African savanna, like other grassland plains, are features of the interior of continents, which are usually dry because they are so far away from the sea. Not enough rain falls to support trees, but hardy grasses thrive on these flat expanses. Some types of grass have roots that extend 5 m (16½ ft) underground in search of moisture. Brush fires often spread across the dry vegetation after a long period with no rain. The ash from these fires nourishes the soil, encouraging more grass to grow when rain falls once more.

Danube Delta

BLACK SEA

Lakes and Rivers

Freshwater features are among the most easily
recognisable landmarks on nearly every continent.
Great rivers and lakes are often dominant features. In this
view of Europe, looking south from high above Scandinavia,
you can see some of the thousands of lakes that cover the
surface of the northern part of the continent. These lakes
were formed during the last ice age, about 10,000 years ago.
The vast glaciers retreated northwards as the ice age came to
an end and temperatures increased. They left behind a
landscape scarred and pitted by the ice. Melting water from
the glaciers, mixed with supplies from springs and rivers,
filled the many "bowls" to form
the lakes that we see today.

The Danube Delta
Europe's second longest river, the Danube
flows for 2,850 km (1,170 miles) from its
source in the Black Forest of Germany to the
Black Sea in Romania. It is
an important river for shipping
because it passes through many
European countries.

- **EUROPEAN LAKES AND RIVERS**
Largest lake: Lake Ladoga, in
the Russian Federation,
18,390 sq km
(7,100 sq miles)
Longest river: Volga, in the
Russian Federation,
3,531 km (2,194 miles)

- **AFRICAN LAKES AND RIVERS**
Largest lake: Lake Victoria,
bordered by Uganda, Kenya,
and Tanzania, 62,482 sq km
(26,828 sq miles)
Longest river: Nile, flowing
through Uganda, Sudan and
Egypt, 6,673 km (4,145 miles)

HEIGHT OF LAND

Above 4,000 m (13,000 ft)
4,000 m (13,000 ft)
2,000 m (6,500 ft)
1,500 m (5,000 ft)
1,000 m (3,200 ft)
500 m (1,600 ft)
300 m (1,000 ft)
150 m (500 ft)
Sea level

▲ **Thick evergreen forests**
surround most of the lakes of
northern Europe and also carpet
the islands that dot these lakes.
The glaciers that carved out the
lake beds during the last ice age
also scraped away at the
landscape so that it is flat as far
as the eye can see.

**This view is looking south
across Scandinavia and
western Russia towards
the Black Sea. The map
below is how this area
is normally shown.**

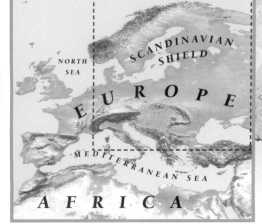

Danube River

Formation of a river delta

The Danube and the Nile, like many other rivers, break down into numerous smaller rivers as they flow into the sea. These smaller rivers fan out to form a triangle shape, called a delta. This term comes from the Greek letter "delta", which is shaped like a triangle. Rivers such as the Danube carry a great deal of soil and silt. When rivers are running fast, especially in the early stages of their journey, they can carry large amounts of material. As they near the sea, however, they slow down so much that they begin to dump the material, and the soil and silt gets deposited, or left behind. Sometimes the deposit blocks the flow of the river, so smaller branches fan out to find a new course to the sea. As these in turn get blocked, yet more branches develop, forming a delta.

1 The original river course. The delta grows as the river deposits silt.

2 New branches develop and the delta grows as more silt is deposited. The river course may alter.

3 Sometimes a settlement grows up around the river mouth and the river's course becomes fixed. The action of the sea wears away at the windward (exposed) side of the delta due to the lack of new silt.

AFRICA

▲ *A satellite picture shows the Nile Delta on the southern coast of the Mediterranean Sea. The green is the rich soil deposited along the banks of the river and forming the delta at the river's mouth.*

▶ *The waters of the Nile and its branches are important for the agriculture of much of Egypt and Sudan, where most of the population live along its banks.*

The Nile River and delta

The Nile River is the longest river in the world. It flows for 4,145 miles (6,673 km) through seven countries in eastern Africa. The Nile begins as two separate branches, known as the White Nile and the Blue Nile. The White Nile begins its course in Lake Victoria in Uganda. The source of the Blue Nile is Lake Tana in the Ethiopian Highlands of the Great Rift Valley. These two branches meet at Khartoum in Sudan. From Khartoum, the Nile River flows northwards through Egypt and forms a huge delta (*see left*) as it empties into the Mediterranean Sea. (*See also pages 23–5.*)

▲ *This wadi runs through Rhoufi in the mountains of southern Algeria, in the heart of the Sahara Desert.*

Wadis

A wadi is a seasonal river, which means that water flows through it only during a period of rain and for a short time afterwards. A wadi appears simply as a dried riverbed at other times of the year when there is little or no rain.

Asia

* **AREA**
  44,680,718 sq km (17,251,315 sq miles). It extends about 10,000 km (6,200 miles) from the Ural Mountains in the west to its eastern tip at the Bering Strait, just across from North America. It stretches another 10,000 km (6,200 miles) from the Arctic Ocean in the north to a string of islands between the Indian and Pacific oceans in the south.
* **LARGEST CONTINENT**
  Asia is the largest of the seven continents, covering about three-tenths of the total land area of the world.
* **POPULATION**
  Approximately 3.5 billion people, including those living in the Asian part of the Russian Federation. More than half of the world's population (57 percent) live in Asia.
* **LARGEST COUNTRY** (by area)
  The Russian Federation (Asian section): 13,177,551 sq km (5,065,451 sq miles)
* **HIGHEST POINT**
  Mt Everest, on the border between China and Nepal, 8,848 m (29,029 ft) above sea level
* **LOWEST POINT**
  Dead Sea, between Israel and Jordan, 392 m (1,2862 ft) below sea level
* **HIGHEST RECORDED TEMPERATURE**
  54°C (129°F) in Tirat Zevi, Israel
* **LOWEST RECORDED TEMPERATURE**
  -68°C (-90°F) in Verkhoyansk, the Russian Federation

The Caucasus Mountains act as a boundary between southwest Asia and southeast Europe. They extend for about 1,200 km (750 miles) from the southwestern shore of the Caspian Sea to the northeastern shore of the Black Sea. The mountains have a great effect on the climate of the surrounding area. They hold the warm, moist air flowing in from the Black Sea and block colder air from the Russian plains from reaching the region.

Asia

You would need to fly high above the Earth to be able to see all of Asia, by far the largest of the seven continents. Here, you are looking down from above the equator, seeing Asia as it stretches northwards towards the Arctic Ocean. Below you, thousands of tropical islands lie between the Indian and Pacific oceans, and the tropical landscape continues up through Southeast Asia. To the west is the Indian peninsula, so large that it is called a subcontinent. Farther west still are the drier regions of the Arabian Peninsula and the Middle East. The climate and landscape changes north of the Himalaya mountains, becoming much colder as the continent stretches farther from the warmth of the equator.

China's great river valleys and western deserts and the mountainous islands of Japan give way to the plains, marshes and forests of Siberia, which extends to the horizon at the northern edge of Asia.

① Himalayas

Taking their name from the ancient Sanskrit word meaning "abode [or home] of snow", the Himalayas are the highest mountain range in the world. They contain not only Mt Everest, the world's tallest mountain, but more than 30 peaks that rise higher than 7,620 m (25,000 ft). The Himalayas stretch about 2,410 km (1,500 miles) in an arc shape across an area of about 600,000 sq km (230,640 sq miles). They form a massive land barrier to the spread of plant and animal species between northern Asia and the Indian subcontinent.

▶ **The exact height of Mt Everest** is the subject of much discussion. Many scientists disagree with the figure of 8,848 m (29,029 ft), which was made with old-fashioned equipment more than 50 years ago.

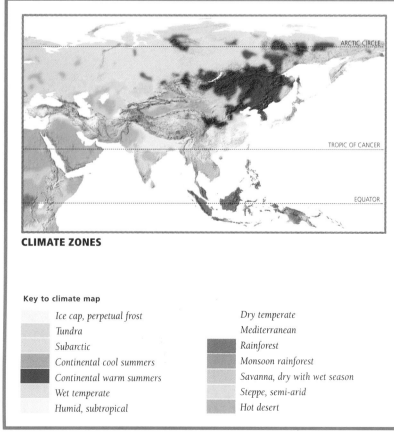

CLIMATE ZONES

Key to climate map

Ice cap, perpetual frost	*Dry temperate*
Tundra	*Mediterranean*
Subarctic	*Rainforest*
Continental cool summers	*Monsoon rainforest*
Continental warm summers	*Savanna, dry with wet season*
Wet temperate	*Steppe, semi-arid*
Humid, subtropical	*Hot desert*

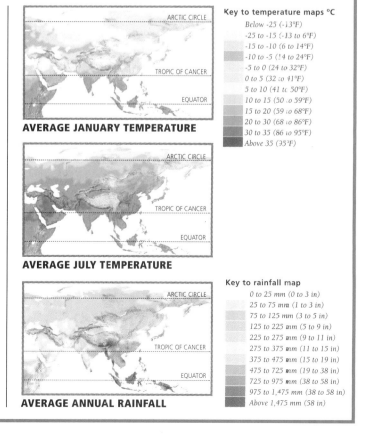

AVERAGE JANUARY TEMPERATURE

AVERAGE JULY TEMPERATURE

AVERAGE ANNUAL RAINFALL

Key to temperature maps °C

Below -25 (-13°F)
-25 to -15 (-13 to 6°F)
-15 to -10 (6 to 14°F)
-10 to -5 (14 to 24°F)
-5 to 0 (24 to 32°F)
0 to 5 (32 to 41°F)
5 to 10 (41 to 50°F)
10 to 15 (50 to 59°F)
15 to 20 (59 to 68°F)
20 to 30 (68 to 86°F)
30 to 35 (86 to 95°F)
Above 35 (95°F)

Key to rainfall map

0 to 25 mm (0 to 3 in)
25 to 75 mm (1 to 3 in)
75 to 125 mm (3 to 5 in)
125 to 225 mm (5 to 9 in)
225 to 275 mm (9 to 11 in)
275 to 375 mm (11 to 15 in)
375 to 475 mm (15 to 19 in)
475 to 725 mm (19 to 38 in)
725 to 975 mm (38 to 58 in)
975 to 1,475 mm (38 to 58 in)
Above 1,475 mm (58 in)

② Siberia

Covering much of northern Asia, Siberia extends from the Ural Mountains eastwards to the Pacific Ocean. Western Siberia is a lowland region with many swamps. To the north, these swamps give way to tundra – marshy plains that are always frozen to great depths. Only the tundra surface thaws briefly in summer, allowing some mosses, plants and shrubs to survive. To the south, the tundra rises gently into a vast evergreen forest belt, known as the taiga, which means "forest-covered mountain" in the local Altai language.

▲ **Some of the coldest winters** on Earth are experienced in Siberia. Its many rivers and streams are locked in ice for up to 10 months a year.

Mt Ararat
5,122 m
(16,941 ft)

Tirat Tsvi
Dead Sea
-392 m
(-1,286 ft)

K2
8,611 m
(28,250 ft)

Mt Everest
8,848 m (29,029 ft)

This view of Asia is looking due north

◄ **Waste from oil** production is simply burned off in flares in parts of the Arabian Peninsula, which has one of the largest deposits of petroleum in the world.

③ Arabian Peninsula

One of the world's driest and least populated areas, the Arabian Peninsula is a huge region of desert that extends southwards from the border between southwest Asia and Africa. It is an immense plateau, covering an area of about 3 million sq km (1.2 million sq miles). The Arabian Peninsula contains some of the largest sandy desert areas in the world, notably the Rub' al Khali (Empty Quarter) in the south and An Nafud in the north. Few places receive more than 7 in (178 mm)

④ Gobi Desert

Lying on a high plateau in China and Mongolia and surrounded by mountain ranges, the Gobi is the northernmost and coldest of all deserts. It stretches 1,610 km (1,000 miles) from east to west and 970 km (600 miles) from north to south. It consists mainly of rolling gravel plains, with low, flat-topped ranges and a few hills. Only the southeastern quarter of the Gobi is completely dry. The remainder has a thin growth of grass, scrub and thorn.

HEIGHT OF DESERTS	HEIGHT OF LAND
13,000 ft (4,000 m)	Above 4,000 m (13,000 ft)
2,000 m (6,500 ft)	4,000 m (13,000 ft)
1,500 m (5,000 ft)	2,000 m (6,500 ft)
1,000 m (3,200 ft)	1,500 m (5,000 ft)
500 m (1,600 ft)	1,000 m (3,200 ft)
300 m (1,000 ft)	500 m (1,600 ft)
150 m (500 ft)	300 m (1,000 ft)
Sea level	150 m (500 ft)
	Sea level

▲The poor soil and dry climate of the Gobi Desert prevent all but the hardiest types of plants, such as these low grasses, from surviving.

KARA SEA

URAL MOUNTAINS

Ob' River

WEST SIBERIAN PLAIN

Ob' River

Yenisey River

S I B E

KULUNDA STEPPE

Lake Balkhash

SAYANSKIY

ALTAI MOUNTAINS

KIRGHIZ STEPPE

BLACK SEA

ANATOLIA

CASPIAN SEA

ARAL SEA

TURAN LOWLAND

KARA KUM

TIEN SHAN

TURPAN PENDI

TARIM BASIN

TAKLA MAKAN DESERT

QAIDAM PENDI

HINDU KUSH

PAMIR

KARAKORAM RANGE

KUNLUN SHAN

IRANIAN PLATEAU

SULAIMAN RANGE

PLATEAU OF TIBET

RED SEA

ARABIAN PENINSULA

PERSIAN GULF

GULF OF OMAN

EMPTY QUARTER

GULF OF ADEN

ARABIAN SEA

Indus River

Sutlej River

THAR DESERT

Yamuna River

HIMALAYAS

Ganges River

Narmada River

DECCAN PLATEAU

CHINDWIN

Godavari River

WESTERN GHATS

EASTERN GHATS

Krishna River

SUNDARBANS

Ganges Delta

Irrawaddy River

Salween River

BAY OF BENGAL

Irrawaddy Delta

SRI LANKA

I N D I A N   O C E A N

ANDAMAN SEA

STRAIT OF

SUMA

NEW GUINEA

Mt Wilhelm
1,534 m (14,793 ft)

CORAL
SEA

TORRES STRAIT

GREAT BARRIER

Cape York

CAPE YORK PENINSULA

ARAFURA SEA

GULF OF
CARPENTERIA

GREGORY RANGE

INDIAN OCEAN

TIMOR SEA

ARNHEM
LAND ③

Mt Stewart
997 m
(3,270ft)

BARKLY TABLELAND

Flinders River

Victoria River

SELWYN RANGE

TANAMI
DESERT

KIMBERLEY
PLATEAU
KING LEOPOLD
RANGES

GREAT ARTESIAN

Mt Zeil
1,531 m (5,023 ft)

MACDONNELL RANGES

SIMPSON
DESERT

LAKE EYRE
BASIN

Diamantina River

Fitzroy River

GREAT SANDY
DESERT

Uluru
867 m (2,845 ft) ①

MUSGRAVE
RANGES

Lake Eyre
-16 m (-52 ft)

Lake Torrens

De Grey River

River

RANGE

LITTLE SANDY
DESERT

GIBSON
DESERT

GREAT VICTORIA DESERT

Lake
Gairdner

Mt Meharry
1,251 m
(4,103 ft)

CARNARVON
RANGE

NULLARBOR PLAIN

ROBINSON
RANGE

④

GREAT AUSTRALIAN BIGHT

DARLING RANGE

Cape Leeuwin

This view of Australia is
looking north-northeast

④ The Nullarbor Plain

The Latin words *nullus arbor*, meaning "no trees", are an appropriate description
of the limestone plain that covers about 300,000 sq km (116,000 sq miles) of south-
central Australia. The Nullarbor Plain measures about 725 km (450 miles) from west
to east and 400 km (250 miles) from north to south. It receives very little rainfall,
and what little moisture there is on the surface tends to disappear quickly. This is
because the limestone allows the surface water to drain down through it, forming
large, water-filled caverns underground. (*See also page 41.*)

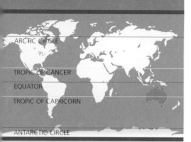

- **AREA**
  7,686,850 sq km (2,967,893 sq miles). It extends about 3,540 km (2,200 miles) from the Indian Ocean in the west to the Pacific Ocean in the east. Its greatest distance north to south is 3,200 km (2,000 miles) from the tip of Cape York in the north to the southernmost part of the island of Tasmania in the south.
- **SMALLEST CONTINENT**
  Australia is the smallest of the seven continents, covering about one-twentieth of the total land area of the world.
- **POPULATION**
  Approximately 18 million people. No other continent, apart from Antarctica, has fewer people. Less than one third of one percent of the world's population lives in Australia.
- **LARGEST COUNTRY** (by area)
  Australia is the only country on the continent.
- **HIGHEST POINT**
  Mt Kosciusko, 2,229 m (7,310 feet) above sea level
- **LOWEST POINT**
  Lake Eyre, 16 m (52 ft) below sea level
- **HIGHEST RECORDED TEMPERATURE**
  53°C (128°F) in Bourke
- **LOWEST RECORDED TEMPERATURE**
  -22°C (-8°F) in Canberra

▲ **The Snowy Mountains** are a southern branch of the Great Dividing Range, and contain the highest peaks in Australia. Glaciers covered the Snowy Mountains during the last ice age, more than 10,000 years ago. They carved out U-shaped valleys and left moraine deposits such as boulders, stones and other debris (*see page 27*). Many of these deposits act as dams to form mountain lakes.

Australia

As you look northwards over the continent, two great bodies of water seem to push into the coast of Australia. In the north is the Gulf of Carpenteria, with Cape York Peninsula on its right. In the south is the sweeping form of the Great Australian Bight, which is like a huge bay across the bottom of the continent. Between and to the west of these vast coastal features is the land known as the Outback, a region of dry land and even desert that makes up most of Australia's interior. To the east of the continent is the Great Dividing Range; the mountainous chain that runs close to Australia's wooded and fertile eastern coast. Lying just south of this coastal stretch is the hilly, forested island of Tasmania.

① Uluru (Ayers Rock)

A massive block of sandstone, known as Uluru or Ayers Rock, rises up from the flat plains in the middle of Australia. Its base measures just under 9.6 km (6 miles) around, and the rock itself rises to 348 m (142 ft), making it the largest single outcrop of rock in the world. Up to about 70 million years ago, Uluru was an island in a large lake, but climate changes drained the waters from the surrounding plains and left the rock exposed to erosion by wind, rain, and changing air temperatures (*see page 41*).

② Great Dividing Range

A system of mountain ranges and plateaus, known as the Great Dividing Range, runs parallel to the eastern coast of Australia. It extends for more than 3,500 km (2,175 miles), from the Cape York Peninsula (the northern tip of Australia) all the way down to the southeastern corner of the continent. The "divide" is between Australia's wooded and fertile Pacific coastal region to the east and the hot, dry interior of the continent to the west, where there is much less vegetation. One branch of the Great Divide continues under water across the Bass Strait and reappears as the central highlands of the island of Tasmania.

③ Arnhem Land

A vast peninsula, known as Arnhem Land, covers an area of about 93,700 sq km (36,200 sq miles) in the central part of northern Australia (*above*). The region is hot all year round and consists mostly of dry woodland on rocky hillsides. Aboriginal people, Australia's first settlers, have lived here continuously for at least 40,000 years; since a time when this part of Australia was still linked by a land bridge to New Guinea. Rising seas gradually cut off this link.

▶ **The Great Dividing Range** consists largely of high plateaus where the height of the land averages about 1,220 m (4,000 ft). These highlands are broken up by steep-sided gorges and valleys.

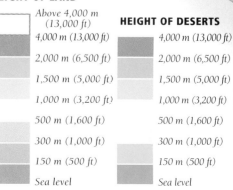

Fortescue
HAMERSLEY
Ashburton River
Gascoyne River

HEIGHT OF LAND

Above 4,000 m (13,000 ft)
4,000 m (13,000 ft)
2,000 m (6,500 ft)
1,500 m (5,000 ft)
1,000 m (3,200 ft)
500 m (1,600 ft)
300 m (1,000 ft)
150 m (500 ft)
Sea level

HEIGHT OF DESERTS

4,000 m (13,000 ft)
2,000 m (6,500 ft)
1,500 m (5,000 ft)
1,000 m (3,200 ft)
500 m (1,600 ft)
300 m (1,000 ft)
150 m (500 ft)
Sea level

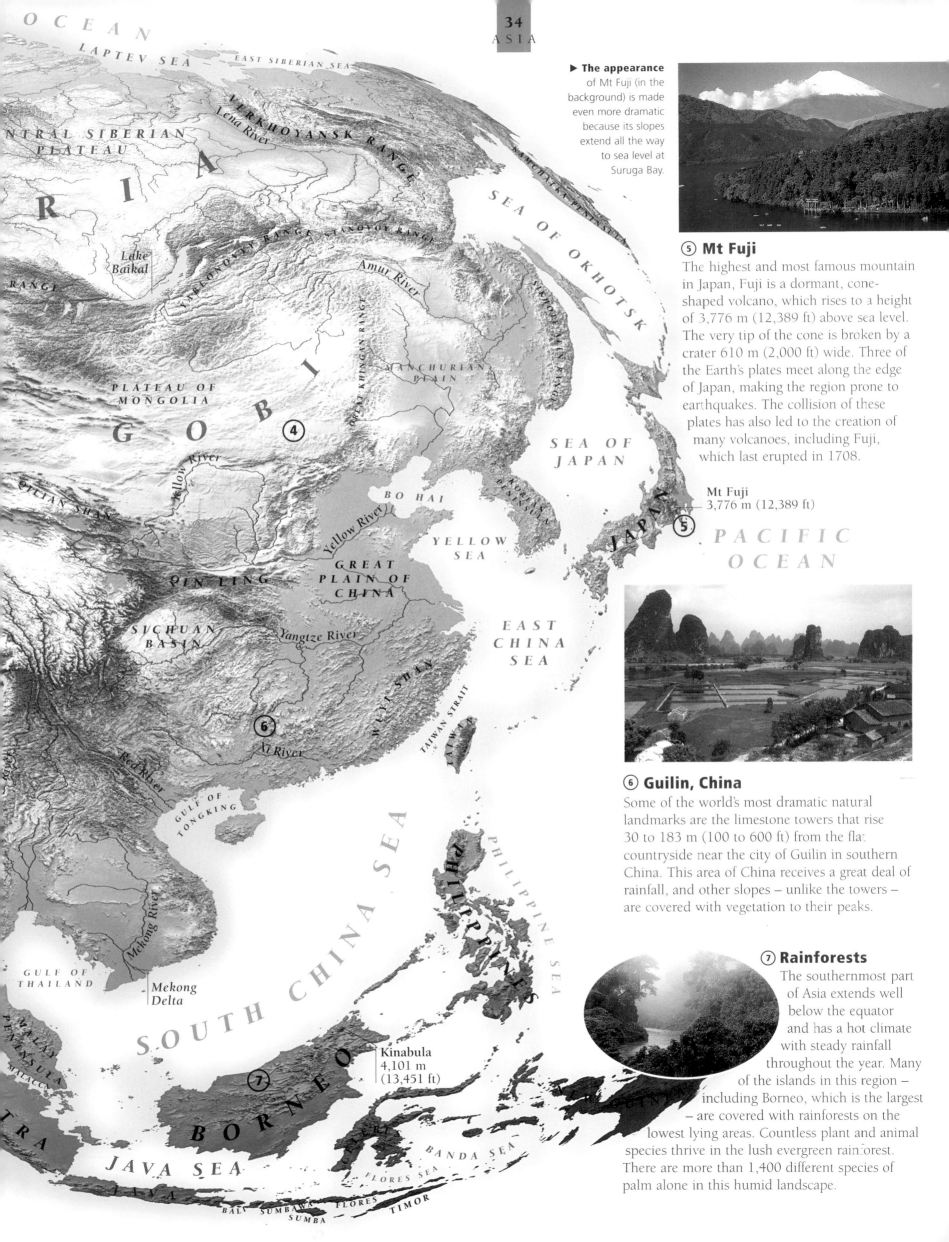

OCEAN
LAPTEV SEA
EAST SIBERIAN SEA
CENTRAL SIBERIAN PLATEAU
VERKHOYANSK RANGE
Lena River
KAMCHATKA PENINSULA
RIA
SEA OF OKHOTSK
RANGE
Lake Baikal
YABLONOVYY RANGE
STANOVOY RANGE
Amur River
SIKHOTE-ALIN RANGE
PLATEAU OF MONGOLIA
GREAT KHINGAN RANGE
MANCHURIAN PLAIN
G O B I
④
SEA OF JAPAN
Yellow River
SILIAN SHAN
BO HAI
KOREAN PENINSULA
JAPAN
⑤
Mt Fuji
3,776 m (12,389 ft)
PACIFIC OCEAN
QIN LING
Yellow River
YELLOW SEA
GREAT PLAIN OF CHINA
SICHUAN BASIN
Yangtze River
EAST CHINA SEA
WU I SHAN
TAIWAN STRAIT
TAIWAN
⑥
Xi River
Red River
GULF OF TONGKING
PHILIPPINES
PHILIPPINE SEA
Mekong River
GULF OF THAILAND
Mekong Delta
SOUTH CHINA SEA
Kinabula
4,101 m
(13,451 ft)
MALAY PENINSULA
TRA
MALACCA
⑦
B O R N E O
NEW GUINEA
CELEBES
BANDA SEA
JAVA SEA
JAVA
BALI SUMBAWA FLORES TIMOR
SUMBA
FLORES SEA

▶ **The appearance** of Mt Fuji (in the background) is made even more dramatic because its slopes extend all the way to sea level at Suruga Bay.

⑤ Mt Fuji

The highest and most famous mountain in Japan, Fuji is a dormant, cone-shaped volcano, which rises to a height of 3,776 m (12,389 ft) above sea level. The very tip of the cone is broken by a crater 610 m (2,000 ft) wide. Three of the Earth's plates meet along the edge of Japan, making the region prone to earthquakes. The collision of these plates has also led to the creation of many volcanoes, including Fuji, which last erupted in 1708.

⑥ Guilin, China

Some of the world's most dramatic natural landmarks are the limestone towers that rise 30 to 183 m (100 to 600 ft) from the flat countryside near the city of Guilin in southern China. This area of China receives a great deal of rainfall, and other slopes – unlike the towers – are covered with vegetation to their peaks.

⑦ Rainforests

The southernmost part of Asia extends well below the equator and has a hot climate with steady rainfall throughout the year. Many of the islands in this region – including Borneo, which is the largest – are covered with rainforests on the lowest lying areas. Countless plant and animal species thrive in the lush evergreen rainforest. There are more than 1,400 different species of palm alone in this humid landscape.

⑤ **The Outback**

Australians use the word "Outback" to describe the vast, flat plain that makes up nearly all of central Australia. It is a hot, dry region that has no forests or lakes and only a few upland regions. Only the hardiest vegetation can survive in the conditions, which range from baking heat during summer days to freezing night-time temperatures during the winter. Some parts of the Outback are deserts, covered either in sand or loose stones (*left*).

⑥ **Great Barrier Reef**

Although its name suggests it is just one reef, the Great Barrier Reef (*above*) is a chain of more than 2,500 smaller reefs. Together they act as a shallow-water barrier stretching for 1,243 miles (2,000 km) between the coast of northeastern Australia and the deeper waters of the Pacific Ocean. The Great Barrier Reef is made up of the skeletons of countless individual corals, which are tiny sea creatures.

⑦ **Tasmanian forests**

The island of Tasmania, lying off the southeastern coast of the Australian mainland, receives more rainfall than any other part of Australia. Tasmania's highest rainfall occurs in the central highlands, which is a continuation of the Great Dividing Range of mainland Australia. A generally mild climate, together with this abundant rainfall, has led to a blanket of thick forests over much of Tasmania. Most of the tallest trees are eucalyptus – more than 600 species of eucalyptus are found on the continent.

▶ **Eucalyptus forests** thrive in Tasmania's abundant rainfall and temperatures that rarely go below freezing.

⑧ **The Murray-Darling River**

Australia's longest river is made up of two rivers, the Murray and the Darling. For much of its course the Murray-Darling passes through countryside that receives little rainfall, so much of the water is lost either through evaporation or by being diverted to supply water for farming. In very dry summers the river cannot even pass the sandbar that has formed across its mouth.

Map labels:
PACIFIC OCEAN
GREAT DIVIDING RANGE
TASMAN SEA
Fitzroy River
Consuelo Peak 1,219 m (3,998 ft)
Round Mountain 1,583 m (5,192 ft)
Lachlan River
Murrumbidgee River
Mt Kosciusko 2,229 m (7,310 ft)
Darling River
Murray River
Barrier Range
Lake Frome
BASIN
REEF
AUSTRALIAN ALPS
FURNEAUX GROUP
BASS STRAIT
KING ISLAND
TASMANIA
Kangaroo Island
Investigator Strait
Spencer Gulf

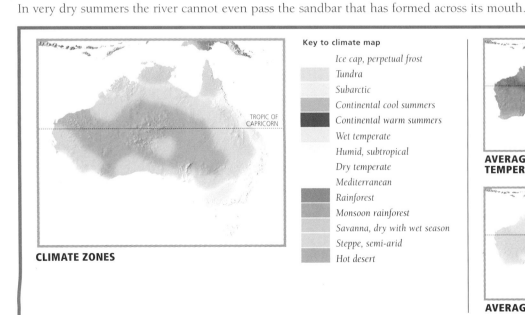

CLIMATE ZONES

Key to climate map

Ice cap, perpetual frost
Tundra
Subarctic
Continental cool summers
Continental warm summers
Wet temperate
Humid, subtropical
Dry temperate
Mediterranean
Rainforest
Monsoon rainforest
Savanna, dry with wet season
Steppe, semi-arid
Hot desert

AVERAGE JANUARY TEMPERATURE

AVERAGE JULY TEMPERATURE

AVERAGE ANNUAL RAINFALL

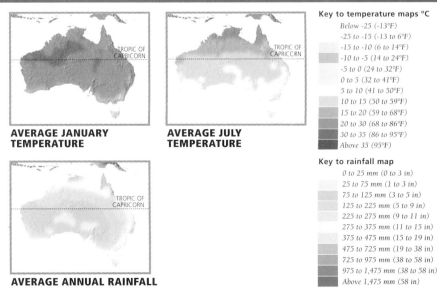

Key to temperature maps °C

Below -25 (-13°F)
-25 to -15 (-13 to 6°F)
-15 to -10 (6 to 14°F)
-10 to -5 (14 to 24°F)
-5 to 0 (24 to 32°F)
0 to 5 (32 to 41°F)
5 to 10 (41 to 50°F)
10 to 15 (50 to 59°F)
15 to 20 (59 to 68°F)
20 to 30 (68 to 86°F)
30 to 35 (86 to 95°F)
Above 35 (95°F)

Key to rainfall map

0 to 25 mm (0 to 3 in)
25 to 75 mm (1 to 3 in)
75 to 125 mm (3 to 5 in)
125 to 225 mm (5 to 9 in)
225 to 275 mm (9 to 11 in)
275 to 375 mm (11 to 15 in)
375 to 475 mm (15 to 19 in)
475 to 725 mm (19 to 38 in)
725 to 975 mm (38 to 58 in)
975 to 1,475 mm (38 to 58 in)
Above 1,475 mm (58 in)

TROPIC OF CAPRICORN

• **ASIAN MOUNTAINS AND VALLEYS**
Highest point: Mt Everest, on the border between China and Nepal, 8,848 m (29,029 ft)

• **AUSTRALIAN MOUNTAINS**
Highest point: Mt Kosciusko, 7,310 ft (2,229 m)

Mountains and Valleys

HEIGHT OF LAND

Above 4,000 m (13,000
4,000 m (13,000 ft)
2,000 m (6,500 ft)
1,500 m (5,000 ft)
1,000 m (3,200 ft)
500 m (1,600 ft)
300 m (1,000 ft)
150 m (500 ft)
Sea level

Looking westwards across Asia, one of the most impressive features is the long chain of mountains known as the Himalayas. Their origins are as dramatic as their appearance. These mountains were once the floor of a sea that lay between India and the Asian mainland. Some 65 million years ago, the plate containing India started to move northwards. It pressed against the Asian landmass, which did not move. Instead, the pressure of the collision pushed the sea floor upwards, forming these huge mountains. The process is still taking place, and the region around the Himalayas often has earthquakes.

Himalayan history

Like most large mountain ranges, the Himalayas were created by the collision of two great plates (*see page 7*). About 200 million years ago, India and Australia were combined on the Indo-Australian Plate, which moved northwards towards the massive Eurasian Plate. On its way, Australia broke off and moved eastwards, leaving India to crash into the southern edge of the Eurasian Plate (*right*). The northern edge of India was forced under the Eurasian Plate, and the seabed between them was folded upwards to form the Himalayas.

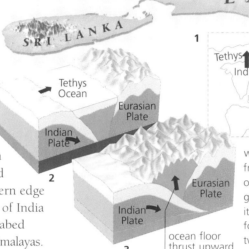

◄ **The Tethys Ocean** once lay between the Indian and Eurasian plates (**1**). The floor of this ocean was covered with sediment that had washed down from the surface of the Eurasian plate over millions of years (**2**). This sediment gradually became sedimentary rock and it was this that was thrust upwards and folded to form the Himalayas when the two plates collided (**3**).

▲ **The Dead Sea** is the lowest place on Earth. At its deepest, the floor is 799 m (2,621 ft) below sea level. The Sea is in fact a salty lake, which has formed in a steep-sided valley at the northern end of the Great Rift Valley (*see page 25*). Plateaus rise to either side. The Jordan River flows into the lake but there is no outlet for the water to escape. The water evaporates, leaving behind large quantities of salt. The Dead Sea is almost seven times saltier than the oceans and its name comes from the fact that no plants or animals can live there.

This view across the Himalayas is looking west, with the great mountain chain dividing India to the south from the Tibetan Plateau to the north. The map below is how this area is normally shown.

The Kamchatka Peninsula and the Ring of Fire

Stretching down from the northeastern tip of Asia is the Kamchatka Peninsula. It is a region of volcanic mountains, and is part of what is called the "Ring of Fire" that circles the Pacific Ocean. Beneath the ocean, the Pacific Plate is constantly moving against the continental plates around it, and the forces of folding and subduction produce many volcanoes (*see pages 6–7*). In Kamchatka, the Pacific Plate meets the Eurasian Plate, which lies beneath nearly all of Europe and Asia. There are 120 volcanoes on the Kamchatka Peninsula alone, and 23 of these are currently active.

AUSTRALIA

Ancient mountains

Although there are many individual mountain ranges running up the eastern coast of Australia, they all form part of a larger system known as the Great Dividing Range. These mountains were formed by the upwards movement and folding of the land, similar to the processes that created the Alps in Europe. But the process took place much earlier in Australia, and the mountains have had many millions of years in which to be worn down by the effects of weather and ice ages. The highest peaks – at about 2,000 m (6,560 ft) – are not as steep as those of many of the world's ranges, and roads lead to the top of them.

▲ ▶ *The Tasmanian Highlands (above) have steep slopes because glaciers cut through these mountains during the last ice age. The Highlands form the southernmost tip of Australia's Great Dividing Range. These mountains prevent damp Pacific air from penetrating the heart of Australia (read about "rain shadows" on page 17) – instead, the moisture is shed over the eastern slopes of the range, providing eastern valleys such as the Hunter Valley (right) with regular rainfall.*

A S I A

PACIFIC OCEAN

INDIAN OCEAN

Turpan Pendi

The most striking feature of the eastern part of the Tien Shan mountain range is the Turpan Pendi (*left*), a 161-km (100-mile) long stretch of lowland that meets a pass leading into the Tien Shan. The Turpan Pendi is the most dramatic example of the deeply folded valleys that were created when the mountains were formed. It reaches 154 m (505 ft) below sea level although it is surrounded by mountains that are up to 6,000 m (19,680 ft) above sea level. These mountains block all rain-bearing clouds from reaching the valley, which resembles a desert.

PERSIAN GULF

IRANIAN PLATEAU

PENINSULA

GULF OF OMAN

ARABIAN SEA

HINDU KUSH

HINDU KUSH

SULAIMAN RANGE

Indus River

THAR DESERT

Sutlej River

Sabarmati River

Chambal River

Yamuna River

Narmada River

PLATEAU

Mahanadi River

GANGES BASIN

Ganges River

Ghaghara River

Ganges River

SUNDARBANS

Brahmaputra River

HIMALAYAS

KARAKORAM RANGE

K2 8,611 m (28,250 ft)

TIEN SHAN

TARIM BASIN

Tarim River

TAKLA MAKAN DESERT

DZUNGARIAN BASIN

Turpan Pendi -154 m (-505 ft)

Mt Everest 8,848 m (29,029 ft)

PLATEAU OF TIBET

KUNLUN SHAN

ALTUN SHAN

QAIDAM PENDI

QILIAN SHAN

CHINDWIN

SHAN PLATEAU

HENGDUAN SHAN

SHALULI SHAN

DAYUE SHAN

WULIANG SHAN

AILAO SHAN

Red River

SICHUAN BASIN

Yangtze River

QIN LING

- **ASIAN PLAINS AND DESERTS**
Largest plain: Great Plain of China, about 1.54 million sq km (600,000 sq miles)
Largest desert: Gobi Desert, in China, 1.28 million sq km (500,000 sq miles)

- **AUSTRALIAN PLAINS AND DESERTS**
Largest plain: Nullarbor Plain, 300,000 sq km (116,000 sq miles)
Largest desert: Great Sandy Desert, 384,000 sq km (150,000 sq miles)

The Olgas are a group of massive rocks that lie just west of Uluru (*see page 35*). Like Uluru, they have been formed by the action of weathering and erosion over millions of years (*see right*). These processes have given the Olgas the shape of several domes – the Aboriginal name for the group is Kata Tjuta, which means "place of many heads". The highest peak, Mount Olga, rises 546 m (1,791 ft) from its base on the plain and the overall group has a circumference of about 22 km (13.6 miles).

This view across Australia is looking east-southeast, almost flipping the view that we usually see of the continent. The map below is how this area is normally shown.

HEIGHT OF LAND

Above 4,000 m (13,000 ft)
4,000 m (13,000 ft)
2,000 m (6,500 ft)
1,500 m (5,000 ft)
1,000 m (3,200 ft)
500 m (1,600 ft)
300 m (1,000 ft)
150 m (500 ft)
Sea level

HEIGHT OF DESERTS

4,000 m (13,000 ft)
2,000 m (6,500 ft)
1,500 m (5,000 ft)
1,000 m (3,200 ft)
500 m (1,600 ft)
300 m (1,000 ft)
150 m (500 ft)
Sea level

PACIFIC OCEAN

TASMANIA
BASS STRAIT
AUSTRALIAN ALPS
Murrumbidgee River
Lachlan River
GREAT DIVIDING RANGE
Darling River
GREY RANGE
BARRIER RANGE
BENDA RANGE
Murray River
FLINDERS RANGES
SPENCER GULF
GREAT ARTESIAN BASIN
Lake Torrens
LAKE EYRE BASIN
Lake Gairdner
Lake Eyre
SIMPSON DESERT
Uluru 867 m (2,845 ft)
MACDONNELL RANGES
MUSGRAVE RANGES
TOMKINSON RANGES
NULLARBOR PLAIN
GREAT AUSTRALIAN BIGHT
TANAMI DESERT
Mt Zeil 1,531 m (5,023 ft)
GREAT VICTORIA DESERT
GIBSON DESERT
Victoria River
GREAT SANDY DESERT
LITTLE SANDY DESERT
CARNARVON RANGE
ROBINSON RANGE
KIMBERLEY PLATEAU
Fitzroy River
De Grey River
Fortescue River
HAMERSLEY RANGE
Ashburton River
Gascoyne River
Murchison River
SHARK BAY
INDIAN OCEAN

ASIA
PACIFIC OCEAN
INDIAN OCEAN
CORAL SEA
AUSTRALIA
TASMAN SEA

Plains and Deserts

As you look down from above the north-western edge of Australia, you see that there is something unusual about this huge island-continent. Compared with other continents, with their large expanses of blue lakes and green plains and valleys, Australia appears to be a mixture of dusty yellows and browns. These are the colours of the deserts and dry landscapes that make up so much of Australia. Nearest us lies the driest part of the whole continent. A series of deserts stretches from the coast below us all the way to the Darling River in the distance.

The Great Sandy Desert

Covering an area of more than 384,000 sq km (150,000 sq miles), the Great Sandy Desert stretches from the interior of Australia out to its northwestern coast. Part of the desert, as its name suggests, is covered in sand. Other areas, however, have a thin, rocky soil, which can collect water from the rare rainfalls. The only significant rainfalls occur when the region is hit by a coastal cyclone, and the rain can be extremely heavy at such times. The only plants that can thrive in conditions that are normally very dry but are subject to sudden floods are tough, clump-forming grasses called spinifex (*pictured above*) and hardy oak trees.

Limestone landscapes

The area along the south central coast of Australia is called the Nullarbor Plain. The Nullarbor is a vast limestone plateau that receives little rain. When rain does fall, the water tends to seep through the limestone, particularly along cracks or faults. Below the surface, it eats away at the rock to create an extensive network of caverns and tunnels (*right*).

▶ **Water seeps underground** from many sources and eats away at the weakest areas of limestone rock to form passages below the surface. It flows through these passages as underground rivers and streams and collects as small underground lakes. As it wears through the rock, it absorbs minerals that form columns called stalactites and stalagmites.

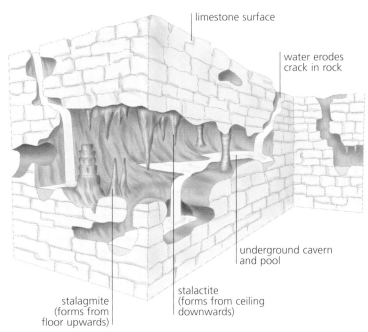

limestone surface

water erodes crack in rock

underground cavern and pool

stalagmite (forms from floor upwards)

stalactite (forms from ceiling downwards)

▶ **Linear sand dunes** form in the Great Sandy Desert following the unchanging direction of the wind. Because the desert is near the coast, the winds tend to come from only one direction – the sea.

Weathering and erosion

Rock is broken down by the process of weathering. There are two types of weathering: physical and chemical. . Physical weathering can be caused by constant changes in temperature that make the rock expand and contract. Water seeping into cracks and then freezing and expanding can also force pieces of rock to break off. Even tree roots and burrowing animals can cause physical weathering. Chemical weathering breaks down rock by slowly altering the minerals that make it up. Rainwater, for example, can mix with carbon dioxide in the air to become a weak acid. Over time, this acid can eat away at rocks. The process of erosion carries away the fragments of rock broken down by weathering. Wind, running water and glaciers can move the fragments huge distances and drop them in landscapes very different to where they started out.

▲ **The Devil's Marbles,** in central Australia, are huge boulders – each balancing on its base. Their shape is a result of onion skin erosion, in which rainwater and changing temperatures weaken surface cracks. The cracks widen, loosening the outer layer, which breaks off in chunks.

ASIA

◀ *Only the northern edge of the Takla Makan, which lies near the Tarim River, has enough moisture to support hardy grasses. In the distance are the Tien Shan Mountains, whose snow-capped peaks are evidence of how moisture-laden clouds cannot deliver rain beyond the obstacle of the mountains.*

Central deserts

By the time moist air from the oceans and seas to the west has reached central Asia, any moisture has been lost over the vast expanses of land in between. Central Asia is made even drier by the fact that the Plateau of Tibet and the Himalayas block any moisture-laden clouds approaching from the Indian Ocean. This lack of water has created two of Asia's deserts, the Gobi and the Takla Makan. It is unusual to have deserts so far from the equator since it is normally hot air currents that create deserts. In fact, the Gobi lies farther north than any other desert and this, together with its height, accounts for its low temperatures at night and in winter. Almost bordering the Gobi to the west is the Takla Makan, the driest desert in Asia. Because it lies so close to the Himalayas, the rain shadow effect (*see page 17*) is extreme. The Takla Makan is a desert of shifting sands. Some of the dunes in its interior rise to heights of about 330 ft (100 m).

ARABIAN SEA

DECCAN PLATEAU

INDIAN OCEAN

GANGES BASIN

DAXUE SHAN

MALAY PENINSULA

GULF OF THAILAND

Mekong River

CHAINE ANNAMITIQUE

Red River

AILAO SHAN

SICHUAN BASIN

GULF OF TONKING

HAINAN

Yangtze Gorges

SOUTH CHINA SEA

WUYI SHAN

Lake Poyang

GREAT PLAI

TAIWAN STRAIT

TAIWAN

Yangtze River

Lake Hongze

Lake Tai

YELLOW

CHEJU-DO

KOREAN

The Ganges is the longest river in the Indian subcontinent, flowing 2,510 km (1,560 miles) from its source in the Himalayas of northern India, to its mouth in the Bay of Bengal. The Ganges Basin is a huge valley watered by the Ganges and its many tributaries. The Ganges Delta is the largest delta in the world and has some of the richest soil.

This view across Asia is looking west-southwest. The map below is how this area is normally shown.

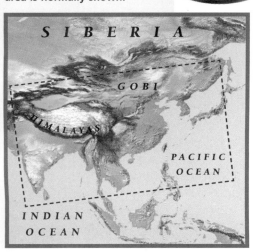

SIBERIA

GOBI

HIMALAYAS

PACIFIC OCEAN

INDIAN OCEAN

Lakes and Rivers

You are high above the Pacific Ocean beyond Asia's coast, looking west across the continent. Ahead of you lie the mouths of two mighty rivers of China. To the north is the Huang He, or Yellow River, which borders part of the Manchurian Plain. Farther south lies the Yangtze, the longest river in Asia – its Chinese name of Chang Jiang means "long river". Both the Yangtze and the Huang He begin their journeys high up in the Plateau of Tibet, where melting ice and snow feed small streams that grow into these great rivers. As they pass through the plains to the east, unpredictable rainfall can sometimes cause them to burst their banks and cause terrible floods.

◀ **The Qutang Gorge** is 900 m (2,952 ft) deep in places. The Yangtze River has been flowing through – and continuing to carve – these magnificent gorges for about 70 million years.

Yangtze Gorges

As well as covering many thousands of miles along its journey, the Yangtze River also descends to sea level from a great height. This drop causes the river to flow very quickly. When it reaches the eastern edge of the Tibetan Plateau, it passes through a 400-km (248-mile) stretch of gorges, which the river has carved out of the landscape (*see page 15*) over many millions of years. There are three main gorges – Wu, Xiling and Qutang – and together they are known as the Yangtze Gorges or Three Gorges.

AUSTRALIA

Groundwater and aquifers

Australia is the driest of all continents; even its largest lakes and rivers shrink during long periods of intense heat and low rainfall. However, there is a great deal of water, called groundwater, trapped below the surface. This water is stored in an aquifer (a layer of rock that is able to hold water within it). The aquifer layer (*right*) is usually sandwiched between two layers of impermeable rock (rock that does not allow water to pass through). Its uppermost layer, near or at the surface, is called the water table. Sometimes, a crack develops in the upper layer of impermeable rock, allowing water to escape (or be pumped) to the surface. Groundwater is an important source of water in many parts of the world, and makes up about 20 times more than the total of surface waters on continents and islands.

▲ *Lake Eyre is a salt lake in south-central Australia. It has formed at the lowest point in the continent and is fed by streams that carry rainwater during the winter rainy season. Its water is salty because so much of it evaporates in the great heat, leaving salts and other minerals behind. In some hot years it dries up completely.*

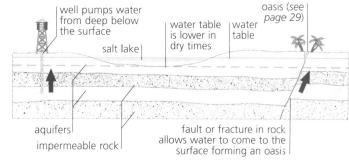

well pumps water from deep below the surface

water table is lower in dry times

water table

oasis (see page 29)

salt lake

aquifers

impermeable rock

fault or fracture in rock allows water to come to the surface forming an oasis

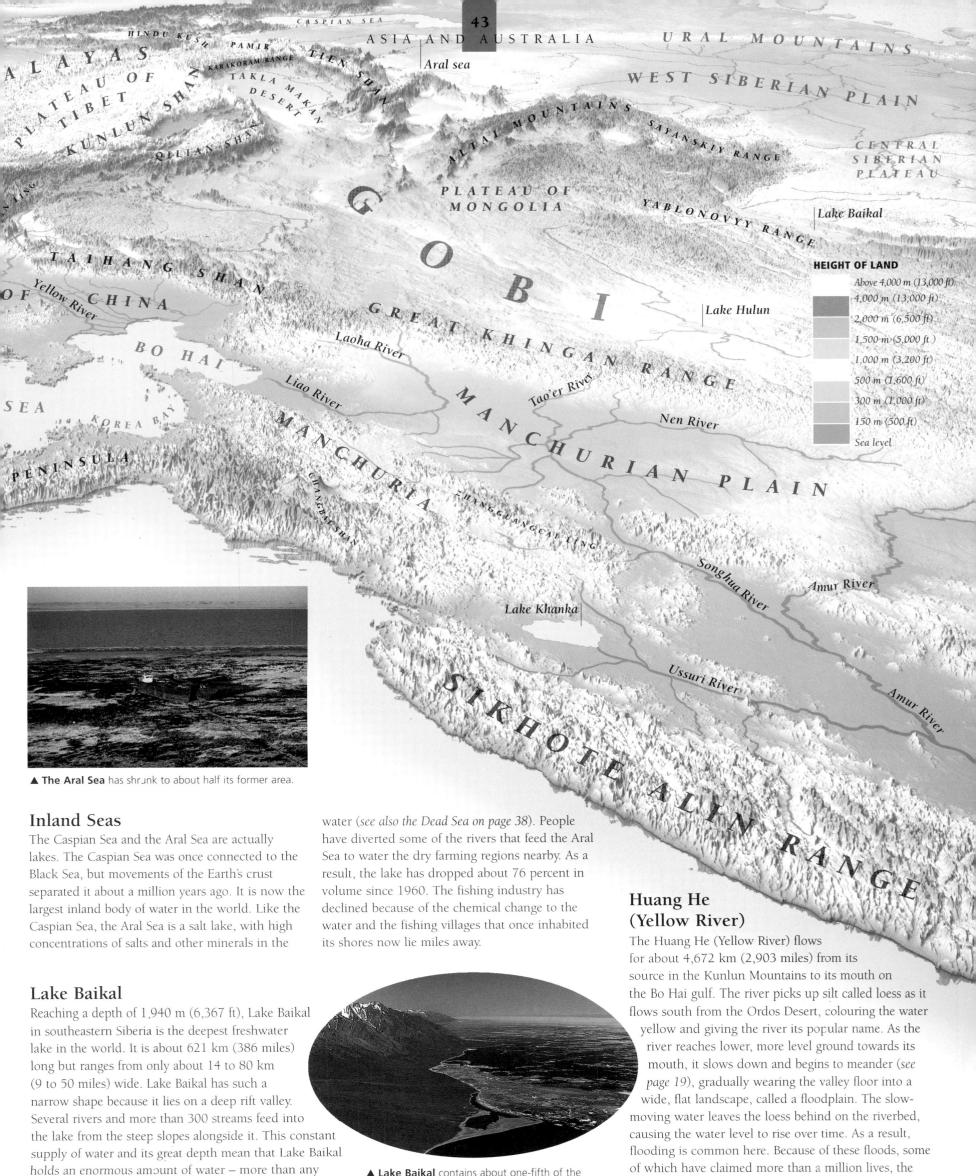

HINDU KUSH   PAMIR   CASPIAN SEA   URAL MOUNTAINS
ALAYAS   KARAKORAM RANGE   TIEN SHAN   Aral sea   WEST SIBERIAN PLAIN
PLATEAU OF TIBET   TAKLA MAKAN DESERT   ALTAI MOUNTAINS   SAYANSKIY RANGE   CENTRAL SIBERIAN PLATEAU
KUNLUN SHAN   QILIAN SHAN   PLATEAU OF MONGOLIA   YABLONOVYY RANGE   Lake Baikal

GOBI

HEIGHT OF LAND
Above 4,000 m (13,000 ft)
4,000 m (13,000 ft)
2,000 m (6,500 ft)
1,500 m (5,000 ft)
1,000 m (3,200 ft)
500 m (1,600 ft)
300 m (1,000 ft)
150 m (500 ft)
Sea level

TAIHANG SHAN   Lake Hulun
Yellow River   CHINA
GREAT KHINGAN RANGE
BO HAI   Laoha River
SEA   Liao River   Tao'er River   MANCHURIAN PLAIN
KOREA BAY   Nen River
PENINSULA   MANCHURIA   Songhua River   Amur River
CHANGBAI SHAN   ZHANGGUANGCAI LING   Lake Khanka   Amur River
Ussuri River
SIKHOTE ALIN RANGE

▲ **The Aral Sea** has shrunk to about half its former area.

Inland Seas

The Caspian Sea and the Aral Sea are actually lakes. The Caspian Sea was once connected to the Black Sea, but movements of the Earth's crust separated it about a million years ago. It is now the largest inland body of water in the world. Like the Caspian Sea, the Aral Sea is a salt lake, with high concentrations of salts and other minerals in the

water (*see also the Dead Sea on page 38*). People have diverted some of the rivers that feed the Aral Sea to water the dry farming regions nearby. As a result, the lake has dropped about 76 percent in volume since 1960. The fishing industry has declined because of the chemical change to the water and the fishing villages that once inhabited its shores now lie miles away.

Lake Baikal

Reaching a depth of 1,940 m (6,367 ft), Lake Baikal in southeastern Siberia is the deepest freshwater lake in the world. It is about 621 km (386 miles) long but ranges from only about 14 to 80 km (9 to 50 miles) wide. Lake Baikal has such a narrow shape because it lies on a deep rift valley. Several rivers and more than 300 streams feed into the lake from the steep slopes alongside it. This constant supply of water and its great depth mean that Lake Baikal holds an enormous amount of water – more than any other lake on Earth.

▲ **Lake Baikal** contains about one-fifth of the world's fresh water.

Huang He (Yellow River)

The Huang He (Yellow River) flows for about 4,672 km (2,903 miles) from its source in the Kunlun Mountains to its mouth on the Bo Hai gulf. The river picks up silt called loess as it flows south from the Ordos Desert, colouring the water yellow and giving the river its popular name. As the river reaches lower, more level ground towards its mouth, it slows down and begins to meander (*see page 19*), gradually wearing the valley floor into a wide, flat landscape, called a floodplain. The slow-moving water leaves the loess behind on the riverbed, causing the water level to rise over time. As a result, flooding is common here. Because of these floods, some of which have claimed more than a million lives, the river is sometimes called "China's Sorrow".

The Arctic and Antarctica

The ice-covered regions around the North and South poles are the coldest places on Earth. Our planet, as it spins in space, is tilted at an angle of 23.5°. This means that the amount of sun that reaches different parts of the Earth's surface changes as the planet follows its year-long path around the Sun. Mapmakers draw an imaginary line around the North Pole called the Arctic Circle and another imaginary line around the South Pole called the Antarctic Circle. The Earth's surface within these circles gets at least one day in the year when the sun never sets and at least one day when the sun never rises! The Arctic and Antarctic regions lie within these circles. The northernmost parts of North America, Europe and Asia jut into the Arctic Circle but the area around the North Pole has no land – it is simply frozen seawater. Antarctica, however, is a continent lying almost totally inside the Antarctic Circle – only the tip of a long peninsula extends beyond the circle.

Frozen seas

Specially designed ships called icebreakers plough through the frozen seawater in Arctic harbours and bays. Salt water freezes at a lower temperature than fresh water, but Arctic winters are cold enough to cause the seawater to freeze to a depth of more than a few metres.

Icebergs

The huge glaciers and ice sheets in both Antarctica and the Arctic are constantly moving, just as glaciers do in a mountain valley. Eventually, they reach the ocean, where they break off to form floating masses known as icebergs. They are often carried away from polar regions by ocean currents, particularly in the North Atlantic Ocean. Some of these North Atlantic icebergs are carried up to 3,200 km (2,000 miles) from their origin. One such "rogue" iceberg caused the *Titanic* to sink off the eastern coast of Canada in 1912.

◀ **All North Atlantic icebergs** form along the edges of the Greenland ice sheet. Many are carried south towards shipping lanes, where they are tracked by the International Ice Patrol.

Mountains of ice

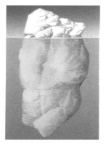

Berg means "mountain" in German, and some icebergs tower 90-150 m (300-500 ft) above the surface of the sea. Water expands when it freezes, becoming less dense, so icebergs float on the water. However, what we see above the water is only part of an iceberg – up to nine-tenths of it extends below the ocean surface (*left*).

▶ **Antarctica's vast ice sheet** produces huge icebergs when its edge meets the ocean. Some of these icebergs are up to 200 km (124 miles) long. Other parts of the sheet remain connected to the continent and form massive floating ice shelves – some as big as France.

THE ANTARCTIC

- **AREA**
  13,209,000 sq km (5,077,540 sq miles). It is mostly circular in shape with the Antarctic Peninsula jutting out towards South America, and with two large indentations, the Ross and Weddell seas and their ice shelves. The thick ice sheets mean that, apart from being the coldest, Antarctica is the highest continent on Earth.

- **FIFTH-LARGEST CONTINENT**
  Antarctica is the fifth-largest of the seven continents, covering about one-tenth of the total land area of the world.

- **POPULATION**
  Antarctica has no native population. Between 1,200 and 4,000 scientists live in the 50 or so bases dotted across the continent.

- **HIGHEST POINT**
  Vinson Massif, 4,896 m (16,063 ft) above sea level

- **DEEPEST POINT OF ICE**
  Wilkes Land 4,776 m (15,669 ft)

- **LOWEST RECORDED TEMPERATURE**
  -89.2°C (-128.6°F) in Vostok Station (lowest in the world)

THE ARCTIC

- **FOURTH-LARGEST OCEAN**
  Arctic Ocean:
  14,351,000 sq km (5,516,524 sq miles)

- **HIGHEST POINT**
  Gunnbjorn, Greenland, 3,700 m (12,139 ft) above sea level

- **LOWEST RECORDED TEMPERATURE**
  -70°C (-94°F) in Nord Station, Greenland

▲ **The Antarctic Peninsula** is the only part of Antarctica where temperatures ever rise above freezing. Snows melt during the short summer, exposing the rocky hillsides of the coast. At the same time, the frozen seawater along the coast breaks up into free-floating smaller pieces.

The Oceans

The Oceans

You are looking north across the world, with the vast Pacific Ocean stretching away beneath you. Most of what you see is blue, showing the expanse of oceans, with island groups dotted here and there. The far-flung islands of the Pacific Ocean are known as Oceania – some of the islands lie within sight of their nearest neighbours, but others are separated by hundreds of kilometres of open sea. The Pacific is the largest and deepest ocean. It covers about one-third of the Earth's surface; together, the oceans cover more than two-thirds of our planet. The ocean floor, however, is part of the Earth's crust, and it is subject to the same faults, rifts, mountain building and volcanic activity as the rest of the Earth's surface.

- **TOTAL AREA OF OCEANS:**
  362 million sq km
  (139 million sq miles)
- **LARGEST OCEAN:**
  Pacific Ocean, 166,241,000 sq km (64,939,000 sq miles)
- **SMALLEST OCEAN:**
  Arctic Ocean, 14,350,000 sq km (5,540,000 sq miles)
- **GREATEST OCEAN DEPTH:**
  Mariana Trench, Pacific Ocean, 11,022 m (36,152 ft)
- **AVERAGE OCEAN DEPTH:**
  3,808 m (12,490 ft)
- **SPREADING PLATES:**
  The oceanic plates are spreading apart – and pushing into the edges of continental plates (*see page 7*) – at a rate of 1–10 cm (0.39–3.9 in) a year.

▲ **Surtsey is a small island** off the southern coast of Iceland. It was formed by volcanic action that began with an eruption in November 1963. Two years later, the lava flow ceased and the island settled into its current area of about 2.5 sq km (1 sq mile). Surtsey is an important research centre for scientists studying how islands form, as well as the types of plant and animal life that are attracted to such a new island. The name Surtsey comes from Surtur, the god of fire in Scandinavian mythology.

This view of the oceans is looking due north

ASIA

AFRICA

RED SEA

GULF OF ADEN

PERSIAN GULF

GULF OF OMAN

ARABIAN SEA

BAY OF BENGAL

ANDAMAN SEA

GULF OF THAILAND

GULF OF TONKIN

SOUTH CHINA SEA

YELLOW SEA

EAST CHINA SEA

CELEBES SEA

JAVA SEA

TIMOR

MOZAMBIQUE CHANNEL

MID-INDIAN RIDGE

NINETYEAST RIDGE

JAVA TRENCH

INDIAN OCEAN

AU

SOUTHWEST INDIAN RIDGE

KERGUELEN PLATEAU

SOUTHEAST INDIAN

SOUTH INDIAN BASIN

ATLANTIC-INDIAN BASIN

SOUTHERN

ANTARCTICA

The Arctic

Unlike Antarctica, the Arctic (*left*) is not a landmass. Instead, it is a giant ice cap resting on one of the world's great oceans – the Arctic Ocean. The ocean is surrounded by the northern edges of three continents – North America, Europe and Asia. For centuries, explorers searched for a Northwest Passage, an ocean "short-cut" between Europe and Asia around the top of North America. We now know that such a passage would have to pass across the permanently frozen expanse of the Arctic Ocean near the North Pole. Submarines have been able to sail across the Arctic Ocean, beneath the covering of ice.

Ice ages

The average temperature of the Earth's surface rises and falls over time, causing great changes to our climate and landscape. Any period during which there are permanent ice caps at the Earth's poles is called an ice age. We are in an ice age right now. When the average temperature drops and remains low for a long time, the ice caps expand and glaciers make their way from each pole towards the equator. Scientists call this a glacial period of an ice age. The last glacial period ended about 10,000 years ago.

◄ During the last glacial period of an ice age, all of Canada, as well as large parts of northern Europe, were covered by the Arctic ice sheet.

PACIFIC OCEAN

SOUTH AMERICA

SOUTHERN OCEAN

ANTARCTIC CIRCLE

BELLINGSHAUSEN SEA

FALKLAND ISLANDS

DRAKE PASSAGE

SCOTIA SEA

AMUNDSEN SEA

ELLSWORTH LAND

SOUTH SHETLANDS ISLANDS

SOUTH ORKNEY ISLANDS

RONNE ICE SHELF

LESSER ANTARCTICA

WEDDELL SEA

SOUTH SANDWICH ISLANDS

MARIE BYRD LAND

BERKNER ISLAND

Vinson Massif
4,896 m (16,063 ft)

ROSS SEA

ROSS ICE SHELF

| South Pole

South Magnetic Pole

NEW ZEALAND

VICTORIA LAND

ANTARCTICA

GEORGE V LAND

QUEEN MAUD LAND

SOUTHERN OCEAN

TASMAN SEA

GREATER ANTARCTICA

WILKES LAND

ANTARCTIC CIRCLE

SHACKLETON ICE SHELF

AFRICA

TASMANIA

DAVIS SEA

AUSTRALIA

SOUTHERN OCEAN

INDIA

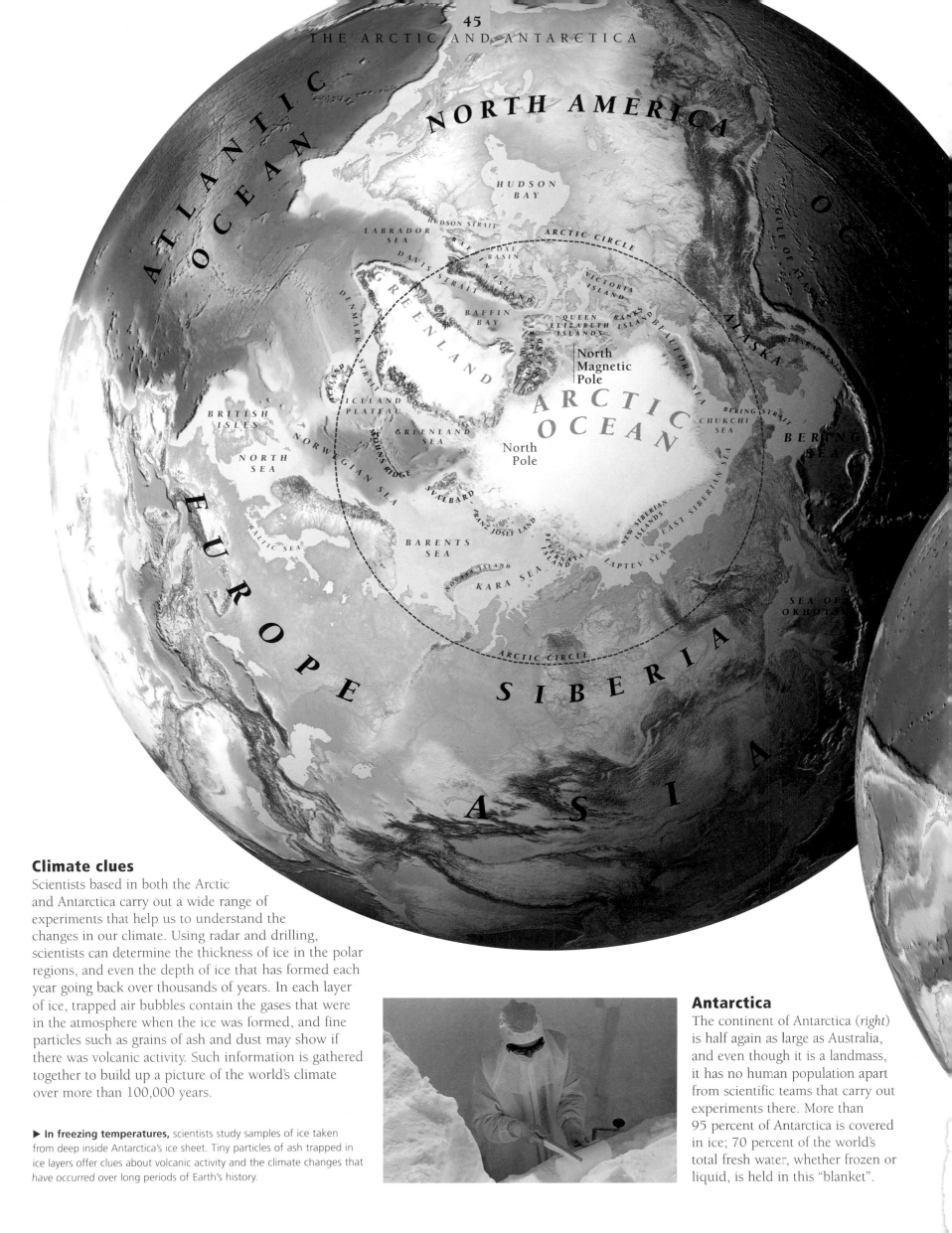

NORTH AMERICA

ATLANTIC OCEAN

HUDSON BAY

HUDSON STRAIT

LABRADOR SEA

DAVIS STRAIT

ARCTIC CIRCLE

FOXE BASIN

BAFFIN ISLAND

VICTORIA ISLAND

QUEEN ELIZABETH ISLANDS

BANKS ISLAND

BEAUFORT SEA

ALASKA

GULF OF ALASKA

DENMARK STRAIT

GREENLAND

BAFFIN BAY

North Magnetic Pole

ARCTIC OCEAN

BERING STRAIT

CHUKCHI SEA

BERING SEA

ICELAND

ICELAND PLATEAU

GREENLAND SEA

North Pole

BRITISH ISLES

NORTH SEA

MOHNS RIDGE

NORWEGIAN SEA

SVALBARD

BALTIC SEA

FRANZ JOSEF LAND

BARENTS SEA

SEVERNAYA ZEMLYA

NEW SIBERIAN ISLANDS

EAST SIBERIAN SEA

SEA OF OKHOTSK

NOVAYA ZEMLYA

KARA SEA

LAPTEV SEA

ARCTIC CIRCLE

EUROPE

SIBERIA

ASIA

Climate clues

Scientists based in both the Arctic and Antarctica carry out a wide range of experiments that help us to understand the changes in our climate. Using radar and drilling, scientists can determine the thickness of ice in the polar regions, and even the depth of ice that has formed each year going back over thousands of years. In each layer of ice, trapped air bubbles contain the gases that were in the atmosphere when the ice was formed, and fine particles such as grains of ash and dust may show if there was volcanic activity. Such information is gathered together to build up a picture of the world's climate over more than 100,000 years.

▶ **In freezing temperatures,** scientists study samples of ice taken from deep inside Antarctica's ice sheet. Tiny particles of ash trapped in ice layers offer clues about volcanic activity and the climate changes that have occurred over long periods of Earth's history.

Antarctica

The continent of Antarctica (*right*) is half again as large as Australia, and even though it is a landmass, it has no human population apart from scientific teams that carry out experiments there. More than 95 percent of Antarctica is covered in ice; 70 percent of the world's total fresh water, whether frozen or liquid, is held in this "blanket".

SEA

EAST
SIBERIAN SEA

BEAUFORT SEA

BERING STRAIT

BERING SEA

GULF OF ALASKA

SEA OF
OKHOTSK

ALEUTIAN TRENCH

KURIL TRENCH

EMPEROR SEAMOUNTS

JAPAN TRENCH

SEA OF
JAPAN

SOUTH HONSHU RIDGE

HAWAIIAN RIDGE

Hawaii

MID-PACIFIC MOUNTAINS

PHILIPPINE
SEA

Guam

MARIANA TRENCH

CLARION FRACTURE ZONE

PHILIPPINE TRENCH

②

CHRISTMAS RIDGE

PACIFIC OCEAN

GALAPAGOS FRACTURE ZONE

BISMARCK SEA

EAS

BANDA
SEA

SEA

① Solomon Islands

ARAFURA
SEA

SOLOMON SEA

CORAL
SEA

STRALIA

LORD HOWE RISE

KERMADEC TRENCH TONGA TRENCH

TASMAN
SEA

TASMAN
PLATEAU

CAMPBELL
PLATEAU

RIDGE

OCEAN

PACIFIC-ANTARCTIC RIDGE

SOUTHEAST PACIFIC

AMUNDSEN SEA

ROSS SEA

ANTARC

① Island chains

Long chains of volcanic islands occur when
volcanoes on nearby continents extend into
the ocean. The Solomon Islands, which extend
1,450 km (900 miles) in the southwestern
Pacific Ocean, were formed in this way. Other
chains, such as the Hawaiian Islands, are
formed when the Earth's crust passes over
"hot spots" of volcanic activity (see page 53).

▲ The relatively still,
warm waters of the
Sargasso Sea encourage
the growth of gulfweed
(*Sargassum*), which gives
the sea its name

② The Mariana Trench

The deepest seafloor depression in the world lies just east of the
Mariana Islands in the western part of the Pacific Ocean basin. The
Mariana Trench is a huge valley that curves northeast to southwest
for about 2,500 km (1,554 miles); its average width is about 70 km
(44 miles). Like many other ocean trenches, the Mariana Trench is
formed by the process of subduction, in which an oceanic plate is
forced down under a neighbouring continental plate (see page 7).
A point near its southwestern end, about 338 km (210 miles)
southwest of the island of Guam, is the deepest place on earth.

GREENLAND
SEA

BAFFIN
BAY

NORWEGIAN
SEA

ICELAND
PLATEAU

NORTH AMERICA

HUDSON
BAY

DAVIS STRAIT

LABRADOR
SEA

DENMARK STRAIT

Surtsey

NORTH
SEA

BALTIC SEA

EUROPE

③ Sargasso Sea

Lying between the West Indies and the Azores, the
Sargasso Sea is an oval section of the North
Atlantic Ocean. It is bounded on the west
and north by the Gulf Stream, a
powerful ocean current that traps
this area of water. Because the
water here is so warm and
relatively calm, large patches
of brown gulfweed grow
on the surface.

MID-ATLANTIC RIDGE

④

Azores

EAST AZORES
FRACTURE ZONE

MEDITERRANEAN
SEA

A F R I C A

③
SARGASSO
SEA

HATTERAS PLAIN

GULF OF
MEXICO

DEPTH OF OCEANS

0–200 m (0–650 ft)

200–2,000 m (650–6,500 ft)

2,000–4,000 m (6,500–13,000 ft)

4,000–6,000 m (13,000–19,500 ft)

Deeper than
6,000 m (19,500 ft)

PUERTO RICO
TRENCH

CAYMAN TRENCH

CARIBBEAN
SEA

DOLDRUMS
FRACTURE ZONE

④

④ The Mid-Atlantic Ridge

Magma flowing up between
oceanic plates cools to form a ridge where
it has poured out onto the ocean floor (*see also
page 7*). Volcanoes often form along the ridge, and
their tops may appear as islands. The
Mid-Atlantic Ridge is a submerged
volcanic mountain range that runs for
about 9,300 miles (15,000 km)
through the Atlantic Ocean. Some
of the mountains break the
surface of the ocean to
become islands, such as
the Azores and
Ascension Island.

MIDDLE AMERICA TRENCH

PACIFIC RISE

ASCENSION
FRACTURE ZONE

Ascension
Island

GULF OF GUINEA

MID-ATLANTIC RIDGE

BRAZIL
BASIN

ANGOLA
BASIN

SAINT HELENA
FRACTURE ZONE

O C E A N

PERU-CHILE TRENCH

NAZCA RIDGE

A T L A N T I C

WALVIS RIDGE

CAPE
BASIN

CHILE RISE

SOUTH
AMERICA

TRISTAN DA CUNHA
FRACTURE ZONE

MID-ATLANTIC RIDGE

ARGENTINE
BASIN

④

ATLANTIC-INDIAN RIDGE

BASIN

DRAKE PASSAGE

SCOTIA SEA

ATLANTIC-INDIAN BASIN

BELLINGSHAUSEN SEA

WEDDELL
SEA

TICA

GREATER ANTARCTICA

South Magnetic Pole

South Pole

TRANSANTARCTIC

PENSACOLA MOUNTAINS

BERKNER ISLAND

RONNE ICE SHELF

Polar Lands

As you swoop down over Antarctica from above the southern tip of South America, the Antarctic Peninsula seems to curl into the heart of the continent. The snow-covered mass of Greater Antarctica stretches off towards the horizon. This is the continent farthest from the equator, and it is very cold, even during summer. Snow never melts on most of Antarctica, and thick ice shelves cover much of the land, stretching into the sea. In the distance, you can see the South Pole – the "bottom" of the Earth – as well as the magnetic South Pole, which is where magnets point when they show a reading of south.

WEDDELL SEA

Graham Land

A great peninsula snakes it way northwards from the main mass of Antarctica. The northern end of the peninsula is called Graham Land, and it is the closest point of mainland Antarctica to any other continent. The southernmost tip of South America lies 1,130 km (700 miles) away, on the other side of the Drake Passage. This body of water opened up when Antarctica finally split from South America about 65 million years ago. Graham Land is also the only part of Antarctica that is north of the Antarctic Circle. Because its climate is relatively mild, compared to the rest of the continent, it loses some of its snow cover in the summer months. This gives scientists an opportunity to examine more easily the rocks that make up Antarctica.

▲ **The rocky surface** of Graham Land is exposed for several weeks each summer. Scientists studying its rocks believe that the Antarctic Peninsula is an extension of the Andes of South America.

JAMES ROSS ISLAND

JOINVILLE ISLAND

• **ANTARCTICA**
Average height: 2,300 m (7,500 ft), which makes it the highest of all continents.
Lowest point: Bentley Subglacial Trench, in West Antarctica, 2,499 m (8,200 ft) below sea level.

• **THE ARCTIC**
Northernmost land on Earth: Oodaaq Island, northern Greenland
Average thickness of ice sheet (on Greenland): 1,500 m (5,000 ft)

▲ **The aurora** is a "curtain" of spectacular lights in the polar skies. It occurs when electrically charged particles, some travelling all the way from the Sun, collide with the Earth's atmosphere. When these bright strings of red and green appear in the northern hemisphere, they are known as aurora borealis (or Northern Lights). In the south, the display is called aurora australis (or Southern Lights).

This view across the Antarctic peninsula is looking south towards the South Pole. The map below is how this area is normally shown.

ATLANTIC OCEAN

INDIAN OCEAN

WEDDELL SEA

ANTARCTICA

PACIFIC OCEAN

ROSS SEA

Moving and stationary poles

The North and South poles are the points around which the Earth rotates. They are known as "geographic" poles. The South Pole is in the heart of Antarctica and the North Pole lies on the frozen Arctic Ocean. The Earth behaves like a giant magnet, with two locations where the magnetic field points directly upwards and not to another place on land. These points on Earth are the Earth's "magnetic" poles. Unlike the geographic poles, the magnetic poles move and have shifted one way then back again more than a 100 times in the last 100 million years.

▲ **Research centres** like this one at the South Pole, allow scientists to study changes that occur over long periods, such as the movement of the magnetic poles.

NORTH AMERICA

1831 1945
1965 1994

GREENLAND

ARCTIC ICE SHEET
• North Pole

SIBERIA

▲ **The North Magnetic Pole** has been approaching the North Pole since scientists began tracking it about 200 years ago. This movement is called polar wandering, but the direction is sometimes reversed along the way.

MOUNTAINS

OSS ICE SHELF

ROOSEVELT ISLAND

Vinson Massif
4,896 m (16,063 ft)

LESSER
ANTARCTICA

ELLSWORTH LAND

Mt Sidley
4,181 m (13,718 ft)

Mt Siple
3,100 m (10,171 ft)

AMUNDSEN SEA

THURSTON ISLAND

BELLINGSHAUSEN
SEA

Mt Jackson
4,109 m
(13,747 ft)

PALMER LAND

ALEXANDER ISLAND

ADELAIDE ISLAND

LARSEN
ICE SHELF

JASON PENINSULA

GRAHAM LAND

ANTARCTICA PENINSULA

ANVERS ISLAND

BRABANT ISLAND

BRANSFIELD
STRAIT

LIVINGSTON ISLAND

SOUTH SHETLAND ISLANDS

KING GEORGE ISLAND

DRAKE
PASSAGE

THE ARCTIC

▲ Moose and elk browse among the short vegetation that covers the tundra each summer. Plants never grow tall because their roots hit ice not far beneath the surface.

Siberian tundra

In the Arctic region, just south of the area of permanent ice to the north is a vast treeless plain called the tundra. Beneath the tundra surface is permafrost, a layer of permanently frozen subsoil in the ground. The soil on the surface thaws in summer, but usually no deeper than about 30 cm (12 in). The combination of frozen ground and flat terrain on the tundra means that it is hard for water to drain away. Instead, it is held at the surface and may drench the upper surface of soil, forming ponds and bogs. Since the tundra receives little rainfall throughout the year, these small bodies of water provide essential water for plants.

▲▶ Cape Prince of Wales, on the Alaskan side of the Bering Strait (above), would have been far from water when the land bridge existed (right).

SIBERIA (ASIA)

ALASKA (NORTH AMERICA)

land bridge

Bering Strait

A narrow body of water known as the Bering Strait separates Asia from North America close to the Arctic Circle. It connects the Bering Sea, which is a northern arm of the Pacific Ocean, with the Arctic Ocean. During the last ice ages up to about 10,000 years ago, ocean levels fell, so that the narrow Bering Strait became a land bridge between the two continents. Many animals, including humans, crossed from Asia to North America at this time.

The Antarctic ice sheet

An enormous ice sheet covers 99.6 percent of the land area of Antarctica. It has formed from the build-up of snow pressing down layer upon layer for more than 100,000 years. In places, this covering of ice is more than 4,700 m (15,416 ft) thick, and its great weight pushes some of the continent below sea level. Satellite photographs have helped scientists to track the ice sheet, which is constantly moving like a huge glacier. "Rivers" of ice moving more quickly than the surrounding sheet flow through valleys and into the oceans.

New Zealand and Oceania

New Zealand and Oceania

As you look north-northeast from a point high above New Zealand, many thousands of islands dot the Pacific Ocean beneath you. This vast area of the Pacific is known as Oceania, and New Zealand's islands are by far the largest of the region. Some of the islands are mountainous, but many others are tiny, with landscapes that hardly rise above the horizon. They are constantly changing, if only slowly – tranquil lagoons now lie where mighty volcanoes once towered, and new islands are growing within the Pacific's famous "Ring of Fire" (*see page 38*).

▲ **The steep slopes of Moorea Island** in the Pacific are covered in vegetation, which thrives on the rich volcanic soil. Surf pounds the fringing reef that stretches around the coast.

Pacific islands

The area of the Pacific Ocean known as Oceania covers about one-fifth of the world and is very different from the rest of the globe. Dotted across this part of the Pacific Ocean are about 20,000 islands, ranging in size from tiny reefs and atolls to the two main islands of New Zealand. In fact, New Zealand makes up more than two thirds of the 390,000-sq km (149,916-sq mile) total land area of Oceania. Pacific islands are either tall and peaked or low and flat, although both were formed by volcanic activity. The peaked islands are nearly all volcanoes. The lower ones are formed partly of coral – these islands were once mountainous, but their immense weight caused them to sink back into the sea.

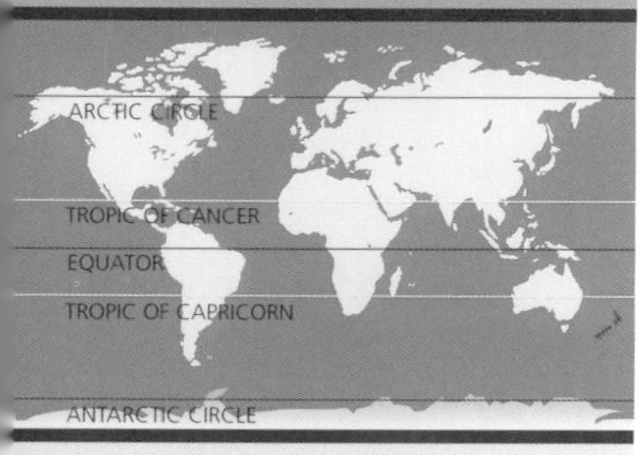

- **OCEANIA**
  Largest atoll: Kwajalein, Marshall Islands, enclosing a lagoon measuring 2,174 sq km (839 sq miles)
  Highest active volcano: Mauna Loa, on the island of Hawaii, 4,169 m (13,677 ft)

- **NEW ZEALAND**
  Highest point: Mt Cook, 3,754 m (12,316 ft)
  Highest waterfall: Sutherland Falls, 580 m (1,904 ft)
  Largest lake: Lake Taupo, 606 sq km (234 sq miles)

Mauna Kea is a dormant volcano on the island of Hawaii – its name means "White Mountain" in the Hawaiian language. Mauna Kea reaches a height of 4,205 m (13,796 ft) above sea level. However, the slopes of the mountain continue 5,998 m (19,680 ft) down to the ocean floor. The combined heights, from base to summit, add up to 10,203 m (33,476 ft), a greater height than any other mountain in the world.

This view across Oceania is looking north-northeast from a point just south of New Zealand. The map below is how this area is normally shown.

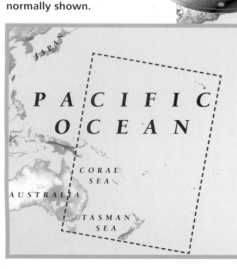

(map labels:) JAPAN · PACIFIC OCEAN · CORAL SEA · AUSTRALIA · TASMAN SEA

(large map labels:) JAPAN · PHILIPPINE SEA · MARIANA ISLANDS · PÖHNPEI ISLAND · NAURU ISLAND · BANABA · MARSHALL ISLANDS · ADMIRALTY ISLANDS · NEW IRELAND · SOLOMON ISLANDS · SANTA CRUZ ISLANDS · NEW GUINEA · NEW BRITAIN · BOUGAINVILLE · SAN CRISTOBAL · ESPIRITU SANTO · EFATE · Mt Wilhelm 4,509 m (14,795 ft) · GUADALCANAL · SANTA ISABEL · MALEKULA · CHESTERFIELD ISLANDS · CORAL SEA · NEW CALEDONIA · AUSTRALIA · TASMAN SEA

Atolls

Low-lying islands, forming a ring that hardly rises above the level of the sea, are known as atolls. Within the ring is a shallow bay called a lagoon, with calm, clear water. Narrow channels may connect a lagoon with deeper waters offshore, but because the ring of land is nearly complete, strong currents and heavy surf never reach the lagoon. Shallow reefs outside the ring also cushion the atoll from heavy seas. Smaller reefs, called fringing reefs, act like stairs, linking the shore to the deeper ocean floor. Larger reefs offshore are called barrier reefs. They were once fringing reefs, but the land behind them slipped deeper into the ocean, leaving them stranded farther from the island. Deposits of a rocklike substance from tiny animals called coral polyps helped to form the reefs.

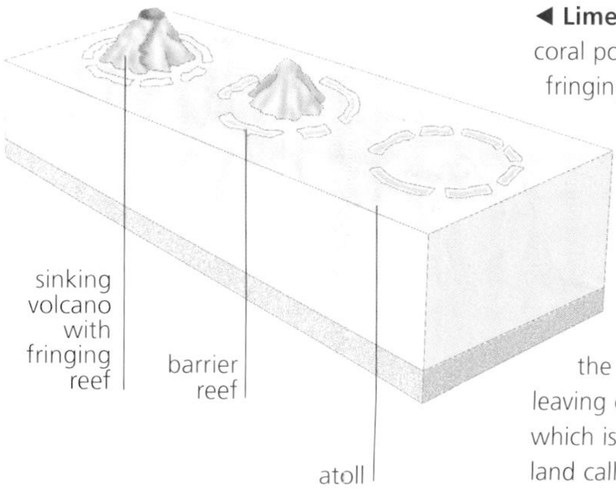

◀ **The form of an atoll** shows up clearly in this photograph of the Pacific island of Palau. The shallow waters inside the tranquil lagoon are visible as a much lighter blue, while the fringing reef is also evident as it slopes outwards into the darkest area of deeper water.

◀ **Limestone deposits** from coral polyps often strengthen a fringing reef, which forms around the edge of a sinking volcanic island. The reef is often left well offshore – as a barrier reef – when the island sinks farther into the ocean. Eventually, the main island sinks, leaving only the original reef, which is now a narrow ring of land called an atoll.

(diagram labels:) sinking volcano with fringing reef · barrier reef · atoll

HAWAIIAN ISLANDS

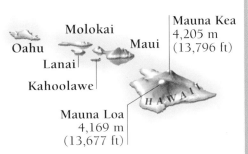

Niihau Kauai

Oahu Molokai
Lanai Maui
Kahoolawe

Mauna Kea
4,205 m
(13,796 ft)

Mauna Loa
4,169 m
(13,677 ft)

HAWAII

▶ *Hawaii, the largest and highest of the Hawaiian Island chain, lies nearest the hot spot that has created the islands. The oldest islands, such as Niihau and Kauai, are to the northwest.*

An island chain

The Hawaiian Islands are examples of hot spot activity (*see right*). They have been formed – and continue to be formed – by the movement of the plate that makes up the floor of much of the Pacific Ocean. This plate is shifting slowly in a northwesterly direction, at a rate of about 10 cm (4 inches) a year. Each of the Hawaiian islands has formed over the hot spot and has then moved to the northeast along with the movement of the tectonic plate. Volcanic activity has long since finished on the oldest islands, which are now slowly sinking back into the ocean.

30 million years ago (mya)

20 mya

10 mya

2 mya

Hot spots

A hot spot is an area of volcanic activity that stays more or less in the same place. The plates of the Earth's crust are constantly moving. When the crust passes over a hot spot the magma bursts upwards to form a volcano. But the plate continues to move so, like an assembly line, the young volcano is pushed along and another one forms above the "hot spot". Gradually the oldest volcanoes begin to sink back into the seabed, forced downwards by their immense weight. Eventually they become atolls.

▼ **A volcano forms** as the plate passes over the hot spot. The plate moves on, and the volcano becomes dormant, with coral forming a fringing reef around it. The island eventually sinks, and only an atoll remains. This, too, sinks as time goes by.

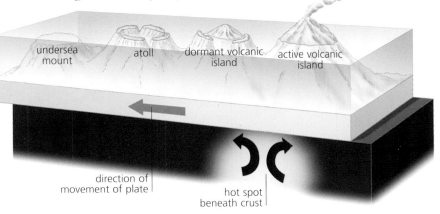

undersea mount

atoll

dormant volcanic island

active volcanic island

direction of movement of plate

hot spot beneath crust

HEIGHT OF LAND

Above 4,000 m (13,000 ft)
4,000 m (13,000 ft)
2,000 m (6,500 ft)
1,500 m (5,000 ft)
1,000 m (3,200 ft)
500 m (1,600 ft)
300 m (1,000 ft)
150 m (500 ft)
Sea level

PACIFIC OCEAN

HAWAIIAN ISLANDS
KAUAI MAUI HAWAII

PALMYRA ATOLL

MARQUESAS ISLANDS

TUAMOTU ISLANDS

COOK ISLANDS

FRENCH POLYNESIA

TAHITI
Moorea

FUTUNA ISLAND
SAVAI'I
SAMOA
ROTUMA
WALLIS ISLANDS
VANUA LEVU
NIUE
VITI LEVU
LAU GROUP
TONGATAPU GROUP

KERMADEC ISLANDS

The Southern Alps

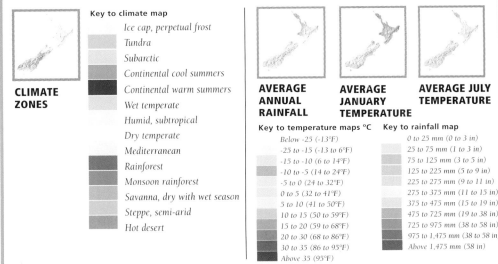

The highest mountains in New Zealand lie in the Southern Alps, which extend about 500 km (312 miles) along nearly the whole length of South Island. Mt Cook, New Zealand's highest mountain, is about midway along the chain. Like several other high peaks, it is covered with snow throughout the year, and there are many glaciers that extend down to the forests below. The Southern Alps create a "rain shadow" (*see page 17*), blocking the path of moist westerly winds. The lands to the west of the mountains receive about 5,000 mm (197 in) of rain each year; those to the east receive only about 500 mm (19.7 in).

Milford Sound

New Zealand has a dramatic landscape, which has been formed and changed by many forces. Most of its highest mountains are either active or dormant volcanoes, and both islands lie on the unstable "Ring of Fire" that runs around most of the Pacific Ocean (*see page 38*). Milford Sound, on the south-western edges of South Island (*pictured above*), is a steep-sided fjord, with snow-capped peaks forming the head of the valley. Glacial activity created Milford Sound and continues to change the landscape of New Zealand.

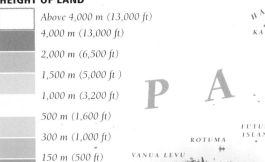

NORTH ISLAND

Lake Taupo

Mt Ruapehu
2,797 m
(9,177 ft)

Mt Cook
3,754 m
(12,316 ft)

SOUTHERN ALPS

CANTERBURY PLAINS

SOUTH ISLAND

Milford sound

STEWART ISLAND

CHATHAM ISLANDS

CLIMATE ZONES

Key to climate map

Ice cap, perpetual frost
Tundra
Subarctic
Continental cool summers
Continental warm summers
Wet temperate
Humid, subtropical
Dry temperate
Mediterranean
Rainforest
Monsoon rainforest
Savanna, dry with wet season
Steppe, semi-arid
Hot desert

AVERAGE ANNUAL RAINFALL

AVERAGE JANUARY TEMPERATURE

AVERAGE JULY TEMPERATURE

Key to temperature maps °C

Below -25 (-13°F)
-25 to -15 (-13 to 6°F)
-15 to -10 (6 to 14°F)
-10 to -5 (14 to 24°F)
-5 to 0 (24 to 32°F)
0 to 5 (32 to 41°F)
5 to 10 (41 to 50°F)
10 to 15 (50 to 59°F)
15 to 20 (59 to 68°F)
20 to 30 (68 to 86°F)
30 to 35 (86 to 95°F)
Above 35 (95°F)

Key to rainfall map

0 to 25 mm (0 to 3 in)
25 to 75 mm (1 to 3 in)
75 to 125 mm (3 to 5 in)
125 to 225 mm (5 to 9 in)
225 to 275 mm (9 to 11 in)
275 to 375 mm (11 to 15 in)
375 to 475 mm (15 to 19 in)
475 to 725 mm (19 to 38 in)
725 to 975 mm (38 to 58 in)
975 to 1,475 mm (38 to 58 in)
Above 1,475 mm (58 in)

AUCKLAND ISLANDS

CAMPBELL ISLAND

Glossary

aquifer A mass or layer of rock holding a large mount of water underground.

arid (of a region) Having very little rainfall making the land dry and able to support little or no vegetation.

atoll A ring-shaped reef left when a volcanic island sinks into the ocean.

barrier reef An offshore reef; the land inside it has sunk into the ocean.

basin A large depression in the Earth's crust; it also refers to an area drained by rivers and tributaries.

bay A part of an ocean or sea extending into the land in a broad curve; it is smaller than a gulf.

billion A thousand million.

canyon A deep, steep-sided valley carved by a flowing river; also called a gorge.

cape The point of a piece of land that juts out into the ocean or other large body of water.

continent One of the seven huge land areas of the Earth: North America, South America, Europe, Africa, Asia, Australia and Antarctica.

continental (of climate) Having distinctly warm or hot summers and cool or cold winters.

delta A triangle-shaped deposit of sediment at the mouth of a river, causing the river to divide into many branches.

desert A region in which the annual rainfall is less than 250 mm (10 in).

dormant (of a volcano) Inactive for a period.

earthquake A movement within the Earth's crust that sends out shock waves when brittle rocks suddenly crack.

equator The imaginary line on the surface of the Earth that divides the planet equally into northern and southern hemispheres.

erosion The transporting away of particles that have been removed from rocks and landmasses because of weathering.

fault A crack in the body of rock.

geyser A vent in the Earth's crust that spouts boiling water at intervals.

glacier A large mass of moving ice.

gorge (see canyon)

gulf A large portion of ocean that is largely enclosed by landmasses.

hemisphere One of two halves of the Earth, usually the northern and southern halves, which lie on either side of the equator.

ice age A period when there are permanent ice caps at each of the Earth's poles.

isthmus A narrow piece of land that links two larger bodies of land.

lagoon A body of water separated from the sea or ocean by a sandbank or a coral reef. A circular lagoon forms inside an atoll.

loess A fine, wind-blown material produced as a glacier scrapes away rocky surfaces.

magnetic pole One of the two locations on the Earth's surface towards which the magnetic needle of a compass will point. They are called the North Magnetic Pole and South Magnetic Pole; at these poles the Earth's magnetic field points directly upwards.

oasis A fertile area in a desert produced when water rises from a crack above an aquifer.

ocean One of the four large bodies of seawater—Atlantic, Pacific, Indian and Arctic—that together cover more than 70 percent of the Earth's surface.

Oceania The name given to all the islands of the central and south Pacific, lying between the Tropic of Cancer in the north and the southern tip of New Zealand in the south and between the southeastern shores of Asia in the west and the western coast of America in the east. Sometimes, the islands of only the south Pacific, including New Zealand, New Guinea and the continent of Australia, are also referred to as Australasia.

peninsula A piece of land that extends into the sea (or an ocean or lake) so that it is surrounded on three sides by water but remains attached to a larger landmass.

plain A large expanse of flat or rolling landscape that has few trees and is often covered with grasses.

plate One of the many large pieces of the Earth's crust.

plateau A broad and mainly flat region of land that is higher than the surrounding regions.

plate tectonics The term used to describe the structure of the plates in the Earth's crust and how they move around and into each other, causing changes to the Earth's surface.

polar Describing the landscape and cold climate of the Arctic and Antarctic regions.

pole One of the two points where the Earth's axis (the imaginary line through the Earth around which it spins) meets the surface. There is a North Pole and a South Pole.

rainforest Vast, dense forest occurring in regions receiving at least 2,000 mm (80 in) of rain a year and supporting a wide variety of plants and animals.

rain shadow The lack of rainfall on one side of a mountain range, occurring because clouds lose their moisture as they are forced up the other side (which receives much more rain).

range Chain of mountains that were formed together by the same forces.

reef A narrow border of rocklike substances that usually builds up because of the activities of animals such as coral polyps.

rift valley A long, deep channel in the Earth's crust that occurs when land sinks along a major fault.

sea An area of an ocean that is almost enclosed by landmasses or by ocean currents.

sediment Particles of soil or rock that have been transported by water, ice or wind.

sedimentary rock A major type of rock formed when sediment and other rocks settle in layers and harden over long periods of time.

semi-arid (of a region) Receiving little rainfall, usually only 250–500 mm (10–20 in) a year.

shield An ancient portion of the Earth's crust that has not been changed by, for example, earthquake activity or folding.

silt Tiny particles of rock that are carried in flowing water.

sound A narrow passage of water between two larger bodies of water or between a mainland and an island.

subarctic Similar to the landscape and temperature just south of the Arctic region.

subduction The process by which a plate in the Earth's crust is forced under a neighbouring plate.

subtropical Describing the climate, landscape and regions bordering the Tropics.

temperate Describing the regions between the tropics and the polar regions, with distinct warm to hot summers and cool to cold winters.

trench A long, steep-sided valley on the ocean floor.

tributary A smaller stream or river flowing into a larger river.

Tropics The hot region on either side of the equator between the tropics of Cancer and Capricorn.

tsunami A giant sea wave caused by an earthquake or volcanic explosion beneath the ocean.

tundra The treeless landscape in polar regions where only hardy grasses, mosses and small woody plants can live; the soil below 30 cm (12 in) down is frozen, even in summer.

undersea mount A mountain that rises from the ocean floor but does not rise above sea level.

volcano An opening in the Earth's crust through which lava, ash, pieces of solid rock and gas are forced out.

weathering The breakdown of rocks on the Earth's surface caused by the action of air, water, chemical substances or changes in temperature.

Acknowledgements

l = left, r = right, b = bottom, t = top, c = centre

PANORAMIC MAPS created by Alan Collinson Design

OTHER ARTWORK: Peter Bull 6–7, 15t, 15 cr, 17cr, 27t, 42br, 53cl, 53cr; Eugene Fleury 5, 15c, 19, 26c, 29c, 31, 38c, 41c, 41bl, 51cr, 52b; Hardlines/Lovell Johns 7t, 46tr; Gary Hinks 44b; Rob Jakeway compasses.

PHOTOGRAPHS: 4c Graham Bush, 4b NASA/www.osf.uk.com; 6tr Galen Rowell/Corbis, 6cl Annie Griffiths Belt/Corbis, 6br The Stock Market; 7cl M.P.L. Fogden/Bruce Coleman; 8tr PowerStock/Zefa, 8c John Cleare/Mountain Camera, 8bl, b Francois Gohier/Ardea, 8/9 Gavin Hellier/Robert Harding Picture Library; 10tr The Stock Market, 10c Richard Hamilton Smith/Corbis, 10cl M. Gottschalk/Britstock-IFA; 11c Francois Gohier/Ardea, 11bl Chris Sharp/South American Pictures, 11b Tony Bomford/www.osf.uk.com; 12tr Sandra Doble, 12bl Francois Gohier/Ardea, 12br Paul Van Gaalen/Bruce Coleman; 13t Staffan Widstrand/Bruce Coleman, 13c Tony Morrison/South American Pictures; 14cl G. Ryan & S. Beyer/gettyone Stone; 15cr Sue Cunningham, 15b Peter Menzel/Science Photo Library; 16l Craig Aurness/Corbis, 16c Annie Griffiths Belt/Corbis; 17tl Robert Harding Picture Library, 17br Tony Morrison/South American Pictures; 18cl Sandra Doble, 18/19 PowerStock, 19tl NASA/Science Photo Library, 19r Fred Mayer/Magnum Photos; 20t J. Allan Cash, 20cl A.P. Barnes/NHPA, 20c PowerStock, 20cr Bob Gibbons/Ardea, 20br Robert Harding Picture Library; 21tl Superstock, 21bl Gunter Graefenhain/Britstock-IFA; 22 J. Allan Cash; 23t Chris Bradley/Axiom, 23cl Christophe Ratier/NHPA, 23c Clem Haagner/Ardea, 23bl Yann Arthus-Bertrand/Corbis, 23br PowerStock; 25t John Cleare/Mountain Camera, 25cr Daryl Balfour/NHPA, 25b PowerStock; 26cl Yann Arthus-Bertrand/Corbis, 26b Adrian Warren/Ardea; 27t Bob Gibbons/Ardea, 28cl James Morris/Axiom, 28c Mark N. Boulton/Bruce Coleman, 28cr Roger de la Harpe/Gallo Images; 29tl Anthony Bannister/NHPA, 29tr Robert Harding Picture Library, 29tcl Gerald S. Cubitt/Bruce Coleman, 29bcl Anthony Bannister/NHPA, 29c Craig Aurness/Corbis, 29b Geoscience Features Picture Library; 30cl Hubert Stadler/Corbis, 31t gettyone Stone, 31b J. Reditt/The Hutchison Picture Library; 32bl David Hamilton/Mountain Camera, 32cr David Paterson, 33t B. & C. Alexander, 33cl Robert Harding Picture Library, 33br The Stock Market; 34tr PowerStock/Zefa, 34cr Robert Harding Picture Library, 34br Jean-Paul Ferrero/Ardea; 35c Hans Christian Heap/Planet Earth Pictures, 35cr Jean-Paul Ferrero/Ardea, 35bl Jean-Marc La Roque/Auscape, 35br Jeff Drewitz/PowerStock/Zefa; 36 Jean-Paul Ferrero/Ardea, 37tl, tr Jean-Paul Ferrero/Auscape, 37br Dennis Harding/Auscape; 38tl Peter Carmichael/Aspect Picture Library, 38c Richard & Julia Kemp/www.osf.uk.com, 38bl, br Jean-Paul Ferrero/Auscape; 39t G. Pinkhassov/Magnum Photos; 40cl, 41t, 41cr Jean-Paul Ferrero/Ardea, 41bl Peter Menzel/Science Photo Library, 41br Peter Carmichael/Aspect Picture Library; 42cl Graham Buchan/Life File, 42cr Michael S. Yamashita/Corbis, 42b Jean-Paul Ferrero/Auscape; 43cl Yann Arthus-Bertrand/Corbis, 43b Richard Kirby/www.osf.uk.com; 44tr, c Corbis, 44bl Mike Jacque/B. & C. Alexander, 44br B. & C. Alexander, 45b J.G. Paren/Science Photo Library; 47cl Bruce Coleman; 48tr Corbis; 50cl B. & C. Alexander, 50cr Dr Eckart Pott/Bruce Coleman, 50b Galen Rowell/Corbis; 51tr B. & C. Alexander, 51br Michael T. Sedam/Corbis, 52tr Nicholas Devore/Bruce Coleman, 52cl Roger Ressmeyer/Corbis; 52br Norbert Wu/Planet Earth Pictures; 53cl W. Jacobs/Trip Photo Library, 53cr Colin Monteath/www.osf.uk.com